The Ribbon of My Life

Pamela Wood

Dedication

*This book is dedicated to believers who, like me,
need a not-so-subtle experience to thrust them forward
in their faith.*

Acknowledgment

First and foremost, I have to thank God. Without His unusual request, I would have remained passive and complacent, safe within my comfort zone. This book is my heartfelt offering to Him, my faithful Lord and Savior.

To Harry, Lucas, Jazz, Nick, and the team at Amazon KDP, thank you for your patience throughout this entire process. I nearly gave up on myself several times, but you never did. Your efforts and encouragement were instrumental in making my vision a reality.

Thank you to my husband, Bob, for providing just the right amount of space and support. I know I wasn't easy to get along with in the overwhelming and stressful moments. Your support means the world to me!

Table of Contents

Preface

God has always spoken in mysterious ways. Throughout history, He has used the most unexpected methods to convey His will, whether through a burning bush, a talking donkey, or even divine handwriting on a palace wall. The Bible is filled with moments where the ordinary becomes the vessel for the extraordinary.

But what if I told you that He still speaks to us today in just as surprising ways? What if His messages are woven into the fabric of our daily lives, hidden in plain sight, waiting for us to see them?

My story is of one such message. It came not through thunder or fire but through a simple ribbon, forgotten, tucked away, and yet imbued with divine meaning. Through this same ribbon, I ventured on a journey of discovery, uncovering lessons that transformed my faith and opened my eyes to reality and life.

This book is not just a story. It is an invitation. As you read, I pray you will begin to see God's hand in the everyday moments of your life. His messages are there. The question is... Are you ready to see them?

Chapter One

The Daily Routine

The warmth of the sunlight spilling through my bedroom window was the first thing I felt that day. Waking up with the first light filled me with a quiet but steady reassurance that this was another gift. I could hear the joyful trill of birds and the soft rustling of leaves through the open window. Stretching my arms overhead, I allowed myself a slow inhale of the cool morning air drifting into the house.

"Thank You, Lord," I whispered, letting the words settle into the hush around me. After a moment, I swung my legs over the edge of the bed and stood, wiggling my toes against the soft rug.

My husband had already left for work, so our home lay calm. This was my time of peace, before the rest of the world stirred. As I entered the kitchen, the comforting aroma of freshly brewed coffee greeted me. I'd prepared it the night before to enjoy without fuss, and it never failed to fill me with warmth and a sense of routine. I reached for my favorite ceramic mug, painted with a bright bluebird perched on a branch, and filled it to the brim with steaming liquid.

I sat at the kitchen table where I'd placed my well-worn copy of Jude, a short but weighty portion of Scripture. Its pages bore fingerprints, notes, and dog-eared corners-tangible tokens of years spent searching its words for guidance and solace. Before reading, I allowed myself a few reflective sips of coffee, my mind drifting from the past etched in Scripture to the changes unfolding in the world around me.

It amazed me how swiftly technology has catapulted us forward: from static rotary phones to sleek smartphones, from black-and-white TVs to instant digital streaming, from dreams of walking on the moon to actual remote-controlled rovers exploring Mars.

"Lord," I murmured, "You've truly given us minds capable of astonishing feats."

And it wasn't just advancements in communication and manufacturing that astounded me. I also marveled at our philanthropic strides in medical research. Many diseases once thought to be unconquerable have been nearly eliminated, and vaccines spare children from devastating illnesses. It warmed my heart to see how caring and resourceful people can be when they devote themselves to helping one another.

I took another slow drink of coffee, then opened Jude. I've always loved this epistle's directness; it calls believers to remain steadfast and cautious of anything that nudges them away from God's love.

"Dear friends, although I was very eager to write to you about the salvation we share, I felt compelled to write and urge you to contend for the faith that was once for all entrusted to God's holy people" (Jude 3). Although centuries old, Jude's message holds a fresh relevance to the world today. As immorality has become mainstream, Christians are faced with a constant choice: compromise or contend.

That phrase, "contend for the faith," felt like a personal challenge: to stand firm in love when tempted to compromise my faith, to uphold the truth of the gospel at all costs. I thought of the modern-day martyrs around the world, who displayed unwavering conviction when it mattered most.

"But you, dear friends, by building yourselves up in your most holy faith and praying in the Holy Spirit" (Jude 20). This was a reminder that growing in faith isn't passive. It requires prayer and intentional acts of obedience and kindness. I wondered if those heroic souls I admired had long nurtured a quiet, prayerful life that readied them for sudden challenges.

"Keep yourselves in God's love as you wait for the mercy of our Lord Jesus Christ to bring you to eternal life" (Jude 21). I read these words slowly. Staying in God's love means choosing empathy over apathy and compassion over indifference. That's precisely what I see in people who step up for others despite any fear that might hold them back.

"Be merciful to those who doubt; save others by snatching them from the fire" (Jude 22-23). A direct call to mercy. If any theme echoes in heroism, it's the swift willingness to help. Whether it's a dramatic rescue or a quiet act of generosity, mercy is the hinge that unites faith with action.

"To him who is able to keep you from stumbling and to

present you before his glorious presence without fault and with great joy" (Jude 24). I felt the promise of God's sustaining hand. He empowers us to do good and ultimately welcomes us into His presence, every fault covered by grace.

Reflecting on that filled me with a renewed sense of peace. Closing my Bible, I exhaled and placed it gently on the table. A fresh wave of gratitude washed over me for these reminders: faith that stands firm, prayer that upholds our resolve, and mercy that bridges our compassion to action.

Bolstered by Jude's encouraging words, I could get on with my day in confidence. As I tidied the kitchen, I couldn't help thinking about stories that inspired me deeply. One such act of heroism involved Jon Meis at Seattle Pacific University. In 2014, amid chaos and danger, Jon, just twenty-two years old and armed with pepper spray, subdued a gunman during a reload, likely saving countless lives. What struck me most was his humility; afterward, he avoided the media spotlight and asked that donations go to the victims. That quiet faith shone through in his actions.

Another story is that of Wesley Autrey. He's the construction worker who, in 2007, dove onto New York City subway tracks to save a stranger suffering a seizure. A train was barreling into the station, yet Wesley pressed the man down in a shallow trench between the rails, and the train passed overhead with mere inches to spare. The media dubbed him the "Subway Samaritan." Still, in interviews, he insisted he did only what he hoped someone else would do in the same situation.

And I recalled how the Boston Marathon bombing of 2013 was met with an outpouring of compassion from runners who pivoted immediately to donate blood or assist the wounded. Local residents welcomed stranded participants into their homes without a second thought. The situation was devastating, but it proved that empathy can flourish even in the grimmest hours.

Sometimes, I marvel at how these heroics align beautifully with Jude's words about mercy and love. It reminds me that faith can be an everyday practice, quietly fortifying us for unexpected moments; that ordinary people choose to live with silent courage and unflinching faith even under the crippling pressure of life.

Even when it's not about heroic rescues, I see the same spirit in a teacher who invests extra hours in a struggling student or a neighbor who organizes a monthly food drive. Though they aren't in the headlines, these heroes embody the same moral impulse to serve others selflessly.

With these thoughts echoing, I left the kitchen and strolled through the living room, collecting misplaced items and straightening cushions. The quiet hum of the refrigerator blended with the distant sounds of a neighbor's lawnmower and a single car passing along our street, each hinting that the world was carrying on. It gave me peace to know that in thousands of homes, people were likely performing the same humble tasks, quietly infused with small acts of kindness and compassion. It reminded me that small acts like these are what drive progress as they urge others to help, heal, and inspire hope in another soul. Whether it is cleaning a room or rescuing a stranger, the good that flows from compassion tends to ripple outward, sparking great advancement. Perhaps this was what propelled all the astounding advances in medicine and charity.

For example, there was a time when polio evoked a sense of terror, leaving children paralyzed or worse. My own mother was a victim of the virus as a child, yet today, millions of children are unaware of that fear, courtesy of a medical breakthrough.

What's more, Jonas Salk, the inventor of the polio vaccine, refused to take a profit from his discovery because he believed it needed to be affordable for all. That is compassion-driven progress in its purest form.

This led me to think of the great humanitarian efforts around the world: volunteers digging new wells in desolate and arid regions; farmers bridging the gap between unused crops and feeding the hungry; and friends using digital platforms to rally life-saving aid within a moment's notice. These are not just a few random acts of kindness. Rather, they are a demonstration of how innovation, guided by compassion, becomes a transformative force.

It is as if, deep within our souls, God set both the inclination to solve problems and the capacity to care-and perhaps His greatest wish is that we would use them together to aid one another.

Eventually, I carried a basket of dirty clothes to the laundry room, loaded the washing machine, and pressed START. The quiet churn of the wash cycle reminded me that even daily chores could become acts of gratitude. I was thankful for appliances that freed me to do more meaningful things, like visiting a neighbor in need.

Passing through a hallway, I paused near a wall of photographs. They captured birthdays, holiday gatherings, and the day my husband and I renewed our vows. Each picture told how family, friends, and even strangers had stepped in to celebrate or comfort. Even in sorrow, when my grandson unexpectedly passed away, I saw glimpses of love: a friend rushing to take care of our lawn; others selflessly volunteering to stay with my three-year-old grandson while we attended his brother's services; a neighbor delivering a warm casserole; a coworker offering an encouraging note; and a church member quietly praying for me.

Not one person expected anything in return. That unstoppable goodness in humankind continues to move me, confirming that our gifts and innovations can be harnessed to serve others.

A phrase that I find myself going back to every now and then is, "Faith can move mountains, but sometimes it also needs human hands to pick up a shovel." It's a reminder that while prayer is powerful, we must also be ready to act. These words, like those of Jude, are a gentle nudge to keep my heart open, prepared to lend a hand or a listening ear whenever needed. I felt an abiding sense that, even in the mundane, daily tasks, God orchestrates opportunities for kindness and compassion. As I stepped outside, I knew that Jude's call to faith, mercy, and steadfast love would guide me through any surprises this day might hold.

Chapter Two

The Discovery

The human brain is a glamorous, chaotic masterpiece. According to some studies, it can generate over one billion thoughts per minute, and yet, despite this endless stream of ideas, you can focus on just 30 to 50 thoughts in a minute. That means, at any given time, your mind is filtering through an avalanche of possibilities, prioritizing what it thinks matters most, discarding the rest into the abyss of forgotten musings.

But what happens to the thoughts you don't focus on? Where do they go? What creates them in the first place? It's as if an unseen force is feeding your mind, allowing you to choose which thoughts you nurture and which you cast aside.

I am often amazed at how you can be perfectly content one moment, then suddenly burdened by a memory, a regret, or a wild, unrelated thought that seems to appear out of nowhere. It's in moments like these that I'm reminded-the mind is a battleground. It is a place where logic fights against emotion, past and present collide, and faith and doubt wrestle endlessly. And yet, despite all the intelligence humanity has gathered, no scientist, researcher, or even the most advanced AI can replicate or fully understand the wonders of the human brain. It is the greatest of all inventions, created by God, capable of storing decades of memories, making split-second decisions, and generating creativity beyond anything programmed into technology. The thought humbled me. How great must the Creator be to craft something as intricate and mysterious as the human mind? And how loving of Him to provide a divine connection to Himself?

Jesus reminds us of this divine connection in John 14:16-17: "And I will ask the Father, and he will give you another advocate to help you and be with you forever-the Spirit of truth. The world cannot accept him, because it neither sees nor knows him. But you know him, for he lives with you and will be in you." If God dwells within you, wouldn't He communicate in ways beyond your understanding? Could the thoughts flowing through my mind that feel inexplicably different be not entirely mine? Could some of them be whispers from God, divine messages that my limited human mind could not fully comprehend?

And yet, despite its brilliance, the mind is restless. It wanders. It pulls you into distractions, whispers fears, and sometimes fills the silence with unnecessary noise. An idle mind is never truly idle. Left unfocused, it will grasp at anything-old wounds, future worries, useless trivia. That's why discipline of thought is so important. The Apostle Paul addresses this very issue in 2 Corinthians 10:5: "We take captive every thought to make it obedient to Christ."

But what if the thoughts that seem random and intrusive

are not actually yours? What if they are whispers from the Divine, nudges placed carefully into your stream of consciousness by God? Could God communicate through the very thoughts you struggle to understand? And what if, in the overwhelming flood of ideas that rush through your mind every second, you lose His voice among the noise?

"How do I slow my brain down?" I muttered, rubbing my temple. A new day had barely begun, but my thoughts were already racing ahead of me, jumping between the list of chores needing to be done, the errands to be run, and the strangely unsettling verses from the book of Jude.

"I felt compelled to write and urge you to contend for the faith that was once for all entrusted to God's holy people" (Jude 3).

The words clung to me in a way that I couldn't shake. I wasn't sure why, but they felt urgent. Heavy. Like they were trying to tell me something I wasn't quite grasping yet. I exhaled, tapping my fingers against the table.

"Lord, what am I missing?" No response. Just silence. And my overactive mind. Then, out of nowhere, a thought emerged- one of those rare, unfiltered thoughts that make you pause mid-sip while enjoying your coffee.

The attic.

I frowned, setting my cup down. "The attic?" It wasn't like I had anything valuable up there-just a clutter of old boxes, furniture, and long-forgotten keepsakes. There was nothing special about it. Nothing that should have popped into my mind at that moment. And yet, the idea sat there, unshaken, refusing to be ignored.

Could it be *God*? Could He be guiding me through something as simple as a thought? Or was my mind just grasping at random ideas? I leaned back in my chair, staring at the ceiling. My brain could have latched onto anything: bills, errands, or laundry waiting to be folded. But instead, it had taken hold of the attic.

Coincidence? Maybe. But my gut told me otherwise. I sighed, standing up.

"Alright, God, if I need to do this, I'll do it. But I expect You to clarify why I'm climbing into a dust-covered time capsule." With a reluctant groan, I trudged down the hall and tugged on the attic pull cord. The ladder creaked as it unfolded, releasing a musty wave of air that smelled like aged wood and forgotten memories.

"Wonderful," I muttered. "Here we go."

The attic was just as cluttered as I remembered: dusty, dim, and filled with the ghosts of past purchases. Old holiday decorations, storage bins, and furniture covered in sheets lined the walls like artifacts from another lifetime. I hesitated at the top of the ladder, waiting for divine intervention to give me some clue as to what I was looking for.

Nothing. Just silence. And dust.

I sighed. "Okay, I'm here. Now what?" My eyes drifted across the room, scanning the boxes until they landed on one in particular-small, tucked away, and unlabeled. That was odd. I always labeled things. Curious, I stepped forward, kneeling in front of it. The cardboard felt worn, the tape barely clinging to the edges. My fingers trembled slightly as I pulled the lid open. Inside lay a stack of children's magazines, a torn teddy bear, pieces from a childhood board game, and... a ribbon.

A shiver ran through me. I didn't know why, but something about it made my stomach twist in that strange, inexplicable way-like when you feel déjà vu but can't figure out why. I picked it up carefully, running my fingers over the mesh-like fabric. Red. Gold-trimmed. Delicate yet firm. It was beautiful, but more than that, it felt purposeful, as if it had been waiting for me all this time. I inhaled sharply. Could this be why the attic had suddenly come to mind? Had this thought been placed there by God, not just to occupy my mind, but to lead me somewhere? Maybe God hadn't spoken in an audible voice, but in the way my brain worked, in a thought so small and simple yet powerful enough that it pushed me to move.

I closed my eyes for a moment, gripping the ribbon tightly.

"Lord, if this is You, help me understand."

The attic was silent, but the weight in my heart told me I had just uncovered something far more significant than just an old piece of fabric.

Clutching the ribbon, I made my way down the ladder, my heart pounding. I didn't know what it meant yet, but one thing was certain. This was only the beginning.

Chapter Three

When the World Forgets

I sat at the kitchen table, staring at the ribbon before me like some ancient relic. My fingers ran over the fabric, the gold beaded trim, and the soft weave of red. It didn't feel special, but I couldn't shake the sense that it was.

I sighed. My brain, the same one that had pulled me toward the attic in the first place, was now a tangled mess of questions.

"Lord, am I overthinking this?" I murmured, staring at the object in front of me. "Is this just some coincidence, or are You trying to tell me something?"

But I heard no booming voice from the heavens, no grand revelation written across my kitchen walls. Just the quiet hum of electrical appliances and the occasional chirping of birds outside. Yet, even in that silence, I felt something stir inside me. A nudge. A whisper. A calling to look deeper.

I reached for my Bible, flipping through the pages with careful fingers. If God were leading me, His Word would offer some clarity. I turned to 1 Peter 1:18-19: "For you know that it was not with perishable things such as silver or gold that you were redeemed from the empty way of life handed down to you from your ancestors, but with the precious blood of Christ, a lamb without blemish or defect." *Blood. Covering. Redemption.*

I glanced at the ribbon again, its deep red color standing out against the oak table. Could this be a reminder of Christ's blood? The ultimate covering, the sacrifice that saved all who believe?

A chill ran down my spine. Was this why God led me to the ribbon? I sat back, my mind racing. If the red symbolized Christ's sacrifice, then what about the gold? Gold was the color of kings, of divinity, and of something set apart and holy.

Another verse came to mind: "The Spirit himself testifies with our spirit that we are God's children. Now if we are children, then we are heirs-heirs of God and co-heirs with Christ" (Romans 8:16-17).

I inhaled sharply. A co-heir with Christ. The weight of that realization pressed against me like an invisible force. I thought of Christ. Not just the name, or the figure we see in paintings, but the living, breathing Son of God who walked this earth. He could have come in the grandeur of a king, robed in gold and seated on a throne. Instead, the Savior came in humility, wrapped in cloths with a manger as His bed... and chose the path of suffering rather than the world's riches.

What kind of love is that? A love so deep that He willingly endured the worst that humanity had to offer: betrayal, mockery, torture. And for what? For me. For all of us. I closed my eyes, feeling the weight of His sacrifice in a way I never had before. The blood of Christ wasn't just an abstract theological concept. It was real. It was pain. It was agony beyond comprehension. The Messiah was beaten, spat upon, and dragged through the streets like a criminal, His body torn apart even before being nailed to the cross.

The cross. I imagined the scene, the darkened sky, the trembling earth, the cries of those who loved Him, and His final words: "It is finished" (John 19:30). They were not spoken in defeat but in victory. The ultimate debt had been paid.

My fingers curled around the ribbon. The red of His sacrifice. The gold of His kingship. A perfect representation of who He is, both suffering servant and eternal King. How could I ever take that for granted?

Tears welled in my eyes. I had spent so much of my life thinking of faith as something distant, something I could grasp when needed and set aside when I didn't. But Christ's sacrifice wasn't just some religious event to be remembered once a year at Easter. It was everything. The moment that changed the destiny of humanity. And here I was, sitting in my kitchen, holding a simple ribbon, yet feeling like I had touched a piece of that sacrifice.

"Jesus, You gave me everything," I whispered. "How could I ever live as if that wasn't enough?"

The thought was sobering. How often had I allowed the world to distract me from what mattered? How long had I chosen my comfort over the call to truly live for Him? I thought of the ordinary disciples who had left everything behind to follow Jesus. They didn't hesitate when He called. They didn't stop to weigh their options. They simply followed. How, then, could I question, doubt, or wait for some grand sign when the most significant sign had already been given? Jesus' sacrifice was enough. It had always been enough.

I wiped at my eyes, exhaling shakily, and prayed, "Lord, help me to never take for granted the sacrifice You made for me. Let me live daily in the truth of Your grace and love."

The ribbon lay in front of me, unchanged, yet distinctly different. It was no longer just a piece of cloth but a reminder, a symbol of everything that mattered: The blood that covered me. The kingdom I belonged to. The Savior who had given it all. I wasn't just looking at a ribbon. I was looking at Grace itself.

But as I held it, letting my fingers run over its delicate threads, a new thought emerged. If Christ had sacrificed so much and given His very life to prove the depth of His love, why did the world seem to reject everything He stood for? Had we not learned anything from His example? Had we indeed fallen so far from His teachings?

I thought about how the world had changed, how humanity had reversed its view of morality. How honesty and integrity, love and kindness had once been the foundation of character but now seemed like remnants of the past, qualities reserved for the naive and the weak.

Once upon a time, honesty wasn't just about telling the truth in small matters; it was a reflection of the soul, of a person's true character. But those days seemed to have disappeared, leaving deception as the norm. Leaders lied effortlessly, manipulating situations and twisting reality to fit their agendas. CEOs robbed shareholders of billions of dollars with no sign of remorse; politicians routinely lied to constituents to retain their positions and power; corporations abandoned life-long employees just as they approached retirement.

Deceit was not limited to the elite. Working-class employees lied on their resumes. Mechanics charged customers for work not completed. Doctors prescribed surgeries for non-existent conditions. Husbands and wives kept secrets from each other. Loyalty had become a weakness to be taken advantage of rather than a virtue to be cherished. Greed had been redefined, not as a selfish desire, but as the "pursuit of happiness."

Though Christ called us to let our 'yes' be 'yes' and our 'no' be 'no' (Matthew 5:37 NKJV), we have created a world where deception and betrayal are not only typical but expected. All for self-promotion and personal gain.

And have we forgotten Christ's call to love one another? "'Love the Lord your God with all your heart and with all your soul and with all your mind.' This is the first and greatest commandment. And the second is like it: 'Love your neighbor as yourself'" (Matthew 22:37-39).

The daily news overflows with stories of violence and crime, but with only an occasional mention of men like Jon Meis and Wesley Autrey. Instead, we hear of mass shootings and acts of terrorism. Of adult children abandoning elderly parents and of human trafficking.

Jesus warned of this in 2 Timothy 3:1-5:

> But mark this: There will be terrible times in the
> last days. People will be lovers of themselves,
> lovers of money, boastful, proud, abusive,
> disobedient to their parents, ungrateful, unholy,
> without love, unforgiving, slanderous, without
> self-control, brutal, not lovers of the good,
> treacherous, rash, conceited, lovers of pleasure
> rather than lovers of God-having a form of
> godliness but denying its power.

The tide has turned so much that displays of love and
kindness are met with skepticism rather than gratitude, and
turning the other cheek is viewed as a sign of weakness. Jesus
received the same treatment. Yet, despite being mocked,
ridiculed, and humiliated, His love never wavered.

I swallowed hard. "Lord, am I truly living for You? Have I
reflected Your love, or have I just been one of the sheep in the
herd?"

The question lingered in the air, unanswered. But deep
down, I knew the truth. I had spent too much time seeking my
own comfort, chasing my own desires, and blending in. I hadn't
cheated anyone or caused physical harm, but Christ didn't
sacrifice Himself so that I could live a life of passive faith.

And what about charity? The words of Matthew 6:2-4
echoed in my mind:

> So, when you give to the needy, do not announce

it with trumpets, as the hypocrites do in the synagogues and on the streets, to be honored by others. Truly I tell you, they have received their reward in full. But when you give to the needy, do not let your left hand know what your right hand is doing, so that your giving may be in secret. Then your Father, who sees what is done in secret, will reward you.

Giving was never meant to be a show. Charity wasn't about earning praise or proving goodness to the world. It was about genuine compassion, about serving those in need without expecting anything in return. But even acts of generosity have become tools for self-promotion. Social media is filled with videos of people "helping" the homeless, always with a camera ready, putting their so-called kindness on display. Jesus warned of the dangers of self-serving righteousness, yet the world has not listened. Many people give only when it benefits them. The wealthy make grand donations to secure tax benefits; politicians use philanthropy as a tool for public approval; and businesses parade their charitable acts to build a reputation.

I stared at the ribbon again. What have we done? Have we forgotten who we are? Are we co-heirs with Christ yet live as if we have no purpose, direction, or understanding?

I shuddered as I recalled Jesus' words in Matthew 25:41-43:

Then he will say to those on his left, 'Depart from me, you who are cursed, into the eternal fire prepared for the devil and his angels. For I was hungry and you gave me nothing to eat, I was thirsty and you gave me nothing to drink, I was a stranger and you did not invite me in, I needed clothes and you did not clothe me, I was sick and in prison and you did not look after me.'

The warning was clear. Those who ignored the suffering of others, those who chose greed over generosity, would face judgment. Still, the world continued on, blind to the consequences.

I looked down at the ribbon in my hands, the red and gold threads woven together in an unspoken message: Christ gave everything. His love, His sacrifice, and His mercy were offered freely. And yet, humanity had turned away, choosing wealth, power, and self-interest over His call to love.

Tears burned at the edges of my eyes. Have I lived a life that reflected Christ's teachings? Or have I taken Him for granted and fallen into the trap of complacency?

"Lord," I whispered, "help me to see beyond myself. Help me to live in a way that honors You."

The world might continue its descent into greed and corruption, but I didn't have to follow. I could choose differently. I could choose truth, even when it is difficult; generosity, even when it is not appreciated; and kindness, even when it is undeserved. Because that is what Christ has done for me, and that is what He has called me to do for others.

Chapter Four

The Power of Redemption

Your Sins Are Covered by Christ's Blood

I've been guilty of dragging up old sins like worn-out records I can't stop replaying, thinking maybe God plays them, too.

My mind sometimes travels back to my younger years in the Air Force. I was just nineteen, stationed in West Berlin-young, untethered, and far from home. It was a time that held more freedom than purpose. And the city, with its buzzing energy and blurred lines, became my playground. Drinking wasn't just tolerated-it was expected. I gave in, trying to fit the mold. I didn't think about who I was becoming or what trail I was leaving behind. I only wanted to belong.

I eventually outgrew that lifestyle, and recklessness gave way to responsibility. But conviction ran deep. Shame lingered like a shadow that refused to leave. Though I knew in my head that I'd been forgiven, it took years for my heart to catch up. That's why I understood, so powerfully, what it meant to grasp for that red ribbon.

I reached out and extended my fingers to it slowly and deliberately. There was nothing physically different about the ribbon, yet I sensed a difference. The color appeared much more crimson now, as if soaking up the dark echoes of whispered prayers, the heaviness of unquiet weeping, and the ache of moments when words failed. In some way, the ribbon wore the essence of mourning and mellowness in its mute presence.

How could something so simple hold such weight? Indeed, it took me back into my past, not to the fragments I chose to remember or the curated memories I recited when asked to give a "testimony," but to the tarnished bits I tried to bury under layers of spiritual busyness. The shame and guilt of mistakes were tucked neatly away like old photographs I didn't want to see but knew exactly where to find. And here I stood face to face with a piece of cloth that felt like God's hand gently pulling the photos out, not to shame me, but to prove-this too is covered.

I remember once thinking forgiveness was a finish line, which I ran toward, panting and breathless, hoping maybe I had made it far enough to deserve it. I thought if I prayed hard enough, served long enough, or gave generously enough, I could tilt the scale in my favor. I lived as if grace was a reward, not a rescue.

That weight, an invisible, oppressive load, hung heavy over my life. No one else could see it, but it was there whispering, "Grace is for the worthy, and you are not."

I was wrong.

But because of that weight, there were times when I dragged myself to church more out of habit than hope. Having little interest, I slipped silently into the back pew, hoping to go unnoticed. But God always found me. Like when the pastor read Psalm 103:12: "As far as the east is from the west, so far has he removed our transgressions from us." He read those words slowly, saying them with that preacher pause that lets the truth settle in. I nodded in approval, trying to seem attentive but recoiling inside. Would God really move *my* sins that far away? Would He really forget what I couldn't?

After the service, I found myself in my car in the church parking lot, unable to move. Tears unexpectedly welled. My fingers trembled against the steering wheel as that verse played through my mind-not a lullaby to soothe but a challenge: He dares you to believe.

And then I voiced a prayer I had been terrified to whisper before. "Lord... help me believe that You have forgiven me. Not that 'church answer' kind of forgiveness, not the kind I quote to others while secretly exempting myself. But real forgiveness. Help me live like I'm redeemed."

This was the beginning, not of perfection, but of peace. And peace is no small thing. It might not always roar. Sometimes, it slips in unnoticed like a blanket gently laid over quivering shoulders, the quiet found in the eye of the storm, or the whispering strength that lets you breathe again when shame tries to silence your song.

Romans 5:9 says: "Since we have now been justified by his blood, how much more shall we be saved from God's wrath through him!" The words are not a theory but a promise. Not a promise dependent on effort or worthiness, resume or reputation, but on Christ's blood. On the crimson cover. A grace that can neither be earned nor deserved but only received. A divine gift was given, not with glitz and glamour but with sacrifice and sacred love.

Just a day after its discovery, that red ribbon, an otherwise worthless cloth, became fully alive with meaning. It was now very personal, as though God had placed it in front of me as a visual sermon: You are covered. Completely. Forever.

And just like that, I needed the reminder. Because even now, there are days when the past is louder than the present. When an old memory rises up like a storm cloud and tries to convince me that I am still that same broken version of myself. For those days, the ribbon is there to reclaim me. It softly but powerfully whispers, "What was once stained with guilt is now crimson with grace." It echoes Hebrews 8:12: "For I will forgive their wickedness and will remember their sins no more."

Do you see it? God not only forgives; He forgets. Not because He has a faulty memory but because His love removes your sins-ALL of them-completely.

This is the *miracle* of redemption. It does not erase the past; instead, it reclaims it. It takes your transgressions and turns them into a testimony.

That red ribbon? It is a banner over my soul. A reminder that even in my worst times, God's grace has already gone ahead of me. And that is the *power* of redemption.

I leaned back as the weight of the message enveloped me. The blood of Christ, shed willingly, in full measure to atone for the sins of the world, had somehow made its way to me. The realization brought a tinge of relief. Like a deep breath that rejuvenates, grace gently loosens shackles that once suffocated. I simply couldn't understand how He could call me beloved while I struggled to call myself anything but broken. Still, Hebrews 8:12 became a holy echo: "For I will forgive their wickedness and will remember their sins no more." Not "again." Not "for now." Not "unless you mess up again." No more.

What once were simply threads in fabric became a thread of hope. A visual reflection of a spiritual truth that often slips through your fingers-especially on the day you feel least worthy. Worthiness is just something grace doesn't wait for. Grace itself creates worth where there once was none.

And so, I held onto that ribbon. Not as an idol, but as a reminder-I am covered. Covered by neither my polished perfection nor my self-made righteousness, but by Christ's. Covered not because I've done everything right but because He did. Covered not in shame, not in silence, not in striving, but in crimson. Redemption is a heavenly covering that not only wipes sin from memory but also transforms the sinner.

Perhaps you have been there too. You may even be there now, carrying invisible guilt that clings to you like a second skin. You smile on the outside while inside, your heart asks, "Will I ever feel clean again?" "Will I ever be free of this guilt?"

May I tell you gently what I had to learn the hard way? Grace is not earned; it cannot be achieved. It can only be received. It's there in front of you. Accept it. Sometimes, we carry burdens God never intended us to carry. We hang on to guilt as if it were penance, as if our suffering made us more deserving of mercy. We drag our shame behind us as evidence-proof that we are truly sorry or that we are still paying for our sin.

But the cross doesn't tell us to carry shame. It tells us to lay it down. I recall one night-quite a long time back-when I sat at the edge of my bed and wrote down all the sins I could remember. I listed the secrets I had hidden for years. Line after line, guilt and shame spilled onto the page, becoming the mirror I never wanted to face. I stared at the words. Tears fell at times, not only out of regret but sheer exhaustion. Why was I doing this? Was it to prove to God how repentant I was? Or maybe I thought He would never forgive me if I forgot.

Then, a hushing thought came. An impression that had no audible sound but felt holy.

Tear out the page and burn it.

The idea seemed melodramatic. Like something you would read, not actually do. Nevertheless, I obeyed. I removed the page, walked to the fireplace, struck a match, and watched the paper shrivel, blacken, and disappear into ashes. Gone.

And at that moment, I realized for the first time: the sin, even the record of sins, wasn't mine to carry. As a child of God through faith in Christ, the moment I took my sin to Jesus, it was forgiven. And when God forgives, He doesn't just mark it off the list; He throws it away. I had known this in my head, but my heart hadn't grasped it until now.

Romans 8:1 offers an even greater promise: "Therefore, there is now no condemnation for those who are in Christ Jesus." None. Not a little. Not a shadow. Not a trace. Christ's blood not only saved me from the penalty of sin, but it liberated me from condemnation.

Do I really believe that? Do I live like that? Or do I keep going back to the ashes, digging up what God already destroyed?

When the enemy whispers my past into my ear, telling me what I did, what I said, where I failed-I don't have to debate him. I don't have to justify or defend my healing. I can stand on the truth: I am justified. I am redeemed. I am made new, for the blood did not miss a spot.

A quiet freedom comes, not when you conquer your shame, but when you stop wrestling with grace and receive it. Not as a theory. Not as a sermon note. But as a covering. A covering soft, crimson, and complete.

As with the ribbon, merely accepting grace may seem much too simple to most of the world. But it is everything to those who know. Just ask the woman in Luke chapter seven.

She remained unnamed, but her story was all too familiar-sinful, scorned, with a reputation that trailed behind her like dust. She stepped into a room where she was neither wanted nor invited, but was desperate to approach Jesus. She offered no argument but simply a jar of perfume and a broken heart.

Kneeling before Him, she wept, washed His feet with her tears, and dried them with her hair. The spectators found this appalling, thoughtless, and disrespectful. But Jesus? Well, He thought it was beautiful. Others certainly ridiculed her. They looked at her as a sinner. But Jesus did not see her as the world did. Where others saw shame, He saw sincerity. Where they saw a sinner, He saw a soul.

In that moment, He didn't measure her past-He received her heart. And in response, He gave her something no one else in the room could: forgiveness.

And for that brief time, the most beautiful words that came from the Lord were these: "Your sins are forgiven. Your faith has saved you; go in peace" (Luke 7:48, 50). Go in peace.

Not "go fix yourself," not "go earn your way back." Just go-freely. In peace-fully.

Those words, falling from Heaven's lips, felt like water on scorched earth. Grace that didn't ask for anything in return. Mercy that outran every accusation. And that... that's the invitation. It has always been.

And that's the matter of this chapter-not only the red ribbon sitting before me but the red thread of redemption that has run through the ages, through every surrendered heart, through every life brave enough to whisper yes to Christ. It's the holy stitch that binds our misery to magnificence.

I can't help but wonder: how many are seated in pews right now, walking down grocery store aisles, driving to work, quietly burdened by shame that God has already lifted? How many wear guilt like a badge, unsure if removing it is even allowed? How many miss the captivating joy of redemption by not believing that freedom truly exists?

Maybe you're one of them. Perhaps you've accepted salvation, but peace is still a stranger. Allow the ribbon to remind you. Let its stain be more than a color. Let it have significance. Let this ordinary object serve as a sermon in thread or a visible whisper that proclaims: no matter how many, how severe or how long ago, your sins are covered.

Not partially. Not conditionally. Fully and completely.

Walk confidently on the ground of grace, for you are not walking alone. You don't need to prove anything. Right now-yes, right now-whether you feel worthy or forgiven, whether your emotions have caught up or your heart still struggles to believe it, the blood of Christ is enough. You are covered.

And that covering? It changes everything.

It doesn't mean you'll never stumble. But it does mean grace will be waiting when you do. It doesn't mean the past never happened. It means the past no longer has authority in your life. It doesn't mean you have reached perfection. It means you are walking in freedom, step by thrilling step.

So, when shame comes crawling back, when the past murmurs once more, and when guilt comes knocking at your door, pick up the ribbon, friend. Hold it close. Let it be more than a memory. Let it be a declaration. A symbol of what Christ has done not only for the world but for you personally. Let it be a constant reminder that redemption isn't a trophy for the disciplined but a rescue for the desperate. You're not too far gone; you're not beyond reach; you're not disqualified. You are no longer bound by sin, but by His grace. No longer held by guilt, but by His mercy. And no longer defined by failure, but by His love-completely and forever in crimson.

Reflection

"Since we have now been justified by his blood, how much more shall we be saved from God's wrath through him!"

(Romans 5:9)

"For I will forgive their wickedness and will remember their sins no more."

(Hebrews 8:12)

Q: What do these verses teach you about what Christ's blood has already accomplished for you?

_____

_____

_____

(Please continue in your own journal!)

Q: How does knowing your sins are forgiven and remembered no more change the way you see yourself?

_____

_____

_____

(Please continue in your own journal!)

Q: In what areas of your life do you still struggle to live as if you are fully forgiven and justified?

_____

_____

_____

(*Please continue in your own journal!*)

Q: How might embracing the reality of being covered by Christ's blood reshape the way you approach God, others, and even your own past?

_____

_____

_____

(*Please continue in your own journal!*)

Prayer

Heavenly Father,

Your word says, "Blessed is the one whose transgressions are forgiven, whose sins are covered. Blessed is the one whose sin the LORD does not count against them and in whose spirit is no deceit" (Psalm 32:1-2).

May I always remember the price Jesus paid on my behalf and never take His sacrifice for granted.

May I always acknowledge and confess my sin to You, knowing You are faithful to forgive. Please help me to accept Your forgiveness and rejoice in You always.

In Jesus' name, Amen.

Chapter Five

Royal Threads

You Are a Co-Heir With Christ

G old is not merely an attractive or shiny object; it solidifies status. It symbolizes wealth, strength, and honor. Gold is the metal flaunted by kings and queens throughout history-symbols of their high standing, their divine right to rule, and the splendor of their kingdom. However, it is not for royalty alone. It is for people who know their real worth and live with the understanding that they belong to something and someone greater. Gold is a reminder that even if you are ordinary, you are precious, valuable, and chosen for royalty.

As I lifted that ribbon again, the gold trim seemed to shine just a little bit brighter, a little more boldly, as if it were summoning me. Like a whisper, it softly breathed, "Remember who you are."

The gold wasn't just an embellishment; it represented something eternal. It was a reminder, a calling to enter into the truth of my identity. Not the identity I give myself, nor the one that the world tries to define for me, but my true identity. The one that's given by the King of Kings. The identity that roots itself in divine love, unshakable grace, and eternal purpose.

The gold told a story of an extraordinary truth: You are a co-heir with Christ. You are not an orphan wandering through the world. No, my friend, you have a seat at the table of the King. You are not meant to live in confusion, striving to live up to worldly standards or to earn your place in life. Your identity is not defined by your past mistakes, by your failures, or by the opinions of others. Your identity is defined by who you are in Christ, and that is where the power lies.

Romans 8:16-17 reminds us of this beautiful truth, "The Spirit himself testifies with our spirit that we are God's children. Now if we are children, then we are heirs-heirs of God and co-heirs with Christ." This is more than just a memory verse to recite in Sunday School. These words form the foundation of an identity that no one can take from you. Hold on to this truth, regardless of what the world throws at you.

The concept of being co-heirs with Christ is mind-boggling. You are no longer a stranger to the King, a distant being with no significance. You have been adopted into the royal family. You belong to the kingdom of God!

This promise is not just for the future, when you will spend eternity in heaven praising and worshipping God. It is also for today. As a co-heir, you have access to everything Christ does. His love, His strength, His grace, and His power are yours. You don't need to prove yourself. You don't need to earn anything. You don't have to strive to gain His approval-you already have it. You only need to receive your inheritance and live in its power.

Understanding this truth changes everything: how you view yourself, how you walk through life, and how you respond to difficulties and struggles. The world will seek to mold your thoughts, to tell you that your worth is based on achievement, and that you are not enough. The reality is that, in Christ, you are more than enough.

Galatians 4:7 reminds us: "So you are no longer a slave, but God's child; and since you are his child, God has made you also an heir."

When that truth sinks into your heart, fear will loosen its grip on you. Insecurities will fade away. You won't feel the need to prove anything to anyone, since you already have the approval of the One who matters most.

Being a co-heir with Christ means embracing what is far beyond what you could ever imagine: the promise of an eternal inheritance. You can, therefore, be confident-not conceited-but quietly confident of who you are in this truth. You can walk tall knowing you do not need to compete with the world or fight for your position; your status is secure because God has determined it.

My heart pounded as the message of that simple gold trim sank in.

"I am a member of the family of God and an heir with Christ," I whispered, thankful for the reminder.

There is peace in knowing your identity is stamped and sealed-that you are loved, accepted, and chosen. Everything you need is complete in Christ, and you can walk through life comforted by the knowledge that your inheritance is unshakable. And that, my friend, is a truth worth holding onto. It's a truth worth living.

To be honest, it has taken my entire life to embrace that fact. I spent many years, even as a Christian, afraid and confused. Self-doubt cast a shadow upon every issue, especially that of identity and self-worth.

You see, at seven years old, divorce took me away from everyone I loved. The very people who gave me my identity were gone. I was no longer a member of the church that loved me. I no longer had the comfort of grandparents or the friendship of cousins. The change left me feeling abandoned, isolated, and alone. Life at home was at times chaotic and uncertain, so I learned to trust only in myself. I thought that if I was 'perfect', I could escape the reputation of the new family I was a part of.

So, I tried to create a new identity through performance. I got all As in school. I obeyed adults without question and followed all the rules. In doing so, I hoped people would see me as my own person-not just as an extension of those around me.

And that's how I lived: constantly trying to prove who I was not but never being quite sure of who I was.

That uncertainty didn't fade with time; it only grew with me.

Years passed, and the need to prove myself lingered, shaping choices and shadowing relationships. By my mid-thirties, I had seen therapists off and on for years, still wrestling with the same drive to measure up. During a counseling session on Wednesday afternoon before Easter, something the therapist said shook me to my core. Referring to my Air Force days, she suggested that I drank "alcoholically" like my mom.

The words hung there, icy and sharp, leaving cold silence. Outwardly, I froze, unable to speak, while inside, I crumbled. My stomach twisted and heat flushed my face. I nodded politely as if to agree with her comment, but in truth, it pierced me like a knife, slicing through the image I had worked so hard to create and leaving me exposed.

As I did each week after therapy, I drove straight to church for Wednesday night prayer meeting. The steering wheel was slick under my palms from sweat, but I held on tightly, thinking I might fall apart if I let go.

On the drive, the therapist's words replayed endlessly in my mind, each repetition like another cut. *Alcoholically. Like Mom.* With every echo, the blade sank deeper, the words less like an opinion and more like a verdict.

And with that verdict came a flood of shame. Every mistake, every bad decision, every time I had let someone down stood in judgment against me. The vow I had made as a teen-to never, ever be like Mom-mocked me. *You are her. You've been pretending. You're no different at all.*

I caught my breath. How could this have happened? Trusting God, believing I could break the mold-it all felt like a waste. In the end, I was seen in the one way I never wanted. My life was worthless. I felt worthless. I accepted defeat.

Then a gentle voice within me whispered, "I'm going to kill myself."

The words surprised me, but they didn't scare me. If I didn't exist, I would be free from defeat or failure. There would be no more wrestling with lies. No more striving to meet expectations-of others, of God, or of myself.

The thought settled in me, steady as the rhythm of breathing. My shoulders relaxed, my mind quieted. Shame, effort, and questions drifted away, sinking into a vast sea of relief. The thought didn't feel wrong; it felt like rest-like an exhale I'd been holding far too long. And I carried that quiet rest with me into the sanctuary.

I slipped into a pew a few minutes early. I watched people shuffle in, heard the soft rustle of hymnals, the murmur of voices. I felt at home, yet strangely distant.

I'll never see these people again, I thought. The words should have stung, but instead they wrapped around me like a soft blanket. No pain, only relief.

I sat there quietly, letting the moments pass as though they belonged to someone else. The songs and prayers drifted by me, empty. I felt both present and absent, seated in the pew yet empty inside, as if my very essence had slipped away. I didn't question the feelings. I simply rested in the emptiness, strangely relieved not to feel the struggle anymore. That relief stayed with me through the service, calm as still water. Yet somewhere beneath that calm, I sensed a subtle, restless undercurrent-a quiet tension I couldn't name.

It lingered even after the last song faded, a whisper that something was not as it seemed.

Only later did the paradox strike me. In just a few days, I was to stand before my church and proclaim the goodness of God in the Easter program. I had planned to speak of His faithfulness and His presence through every season of my life. Yet I almost let deception pull me from His presence, mistaking the path of death for the promise of life.

How could I be so quickly deceived? How could despair look so much like peace?

The answer was disturbing but undeniable: it was Satan's deception. He blurred my vision just enough to make his lies appear as truth. He made hopelessness look like peace, but in reality, it was nothing more than the absence of fight.

Realizing how easily I had welcomed the lie humbled me and left me deeply unsettled, even afraid of my own capacity to be deceived. It was clear that I had not taken my seat at the table with Christ, that I had not grasped my true identity as a child of God. The scary thing is, I believed that I was a strong Christian and not vulnerable to Satan's attacks. How wrong I was! Satan saw my weakness and pounced. Blindsided, I fell into confusion and despair.

Thankfully, God responded just as quickly as Satan had attacked. The testimony I had prepared detailed the presence of God's love, His mercy, and His grace throughout my life. Reading my testimony again dispelled the confusion. I clearly saw that I was not who others thought I was, and that the opinions of others meant nothing. Possibly for the first time, I began to fully understand that my identity and self-worth are based not on my family, my failures, or my accomplishments. They are rooted in my relationship with Christ alone.

That realization gave shape to the relief I had once felt in the sanctuary. The calm was the same, but now it was no illusion. This time it was rooted in truth, not lies. I had everything I wanted and needed in Christ.

Yet even with that freedom, I learned that maintaining this identity is a constant battle. It requires consciously capturing the lies that haunt my mind and exchanging them for the truth of who I am in Christ. It is a process of choosing daily, on every occasion, to walk in the freedom that comes from accepting my place in God's kingdom. Now, when I say to myself, "I am a child of the King," I believe it.

If you lose sight of who you are-and you likely will-you are not alone. We all have moments of weakness. Peter denied knowing Jesus, Moses was insecure, Gideon thought he was too weak for the job, and Jeremiah doubted his abilities.

When your identity or self-worth wanes, there are steps you

can take to reclaim your position.

Remind Yourself of Who You Are

It sounds simple, but it requires constant effort. The world will try to tear you down, but don't let worldly thoughts take root. Refresh your mind with these Bible verses daily to help you stand firm in times of weakness:

1 Peter 2:9: "But you are a chosen people, a royal priesthood, a holy nation, God's special possession, that you may declare the praises of him who called you out of darkness into his wonderful light."

Your identity is not accidental. You belong to God.

John 1:12: "Yet to all who did receive him, to those who believed in his name, he gave the right to become children of God."

You belong simply because you believe.

Galatians 3:26-27: "So in Christ Jesus you are all children of God through faith, for all of you who were baptized into Christ have clothed yourselves with Christ."

You are clothed in Christ's righteousness and made new.

Walk in Confidence

Once you know your identity, own it. Accept it. Live in it

daily.

Romans 8:31: "If God is for us, who can be against us?"

Nothing and no one can stand in the way of God's plan for you.

Philippians 1:6: "being confident of this, that he who began a good work in you will carry it on to completion until the day of Christ Jesus."

Your growth and purpose are secure in His hands.

Philippians 4:13: "I can do all this through him who gives me strength."

You are equipped and empowered to live boldly.

Live Like a Child of God

Romans 12 is an excellent guide for how to treat others. It tells us to serve and encourage one another; to give generously and to cheerfully show mercy. The passage also exhorts us to love one another and to honor others above ourselves. Finally, it commands us to live at peace with others, to put aside pride, and to leave vengeance to God. I read this chapter often to keep my attitude in check. Just imagine what the world would be like if we all followed this model!

Rest in Your Inheritance

Stop striving! You don't have to prove yourself. Being a co-heir means that you are forgiven and redeemed. Your position as His child is assured. Your inheritance is unbreakable, unchangeable, everlasting, and will never lose its value. It is secure now and forever.

Reclaiming your identity isn't about trying harder-it's about remembering what is already true. When you remind yourself of God's Word, walk with the quiet confidence of His promises, live as His child, and rest in your inheritance, you no longer have to chase approval or fear rejection. You can breathe easier, knowing your worth is settled, your place is secure, and your name is written in heaven. That is who you are. That is the identity no one can take away.

Reflection

"If you belong to Christ, then you are Abraham's seed, and heirs according to the promise."

(Galatians 3:29)

"So in Christ Jesus you are all children of God through faith."

(Galatians 3:26)

Q: What does it mean to "belong to Christ" in the context of this verse?

_____
_____
_____

(Please continue in your own journal!)

Q: How does being called Abraham's seed connect you to God's story of faith throughout Scripture?

_____
_____
_____

(Please continue in your own journal!)

Q: What promises of God do you find it hardest to fully claim as your inheritance in Christ?

_____

_____

_____

(Please continue in your own journal!)

Q: How might living daily as an heir of God's promises change the way you see your identity, purpose, and future?

_____

_____

_____

(Please continue in your own journal!)

Prayer

Heavenly Father,

I come before You in the name of Jesus, recognizing that I am Your child and a co-heir with Christ. Thank You for the incredible gift of salvation and the promise of an eternal inheritance. Help me to live in the reality of this truth, walking in the power and authority that You have given me as Your child. May I live each day with a joyful expectation of the blessings You have promised.

In the precious name of Jesus, Amen.

Chapter Six

Yielding to God's Hands

You Must Be Willing to Be Molded by God

There are different types of ribbon. Some are made of material that is soft, flexible, and pliable, while others are stiff and retain their shape and structure.

The softer ribbon actually resigns itself to the hand that shapes it. It doesn't resist or fight back. It doesn't need to show strength by holding onto its form. This ribbon submits to the bending, gracefully allowing itself to be folded, twisted, or tied into new shapes, and still... it remains beautiful.

The essence of the ribbon is not lost in the bending. Rather, the ribbon's very purpose seems to be revealed through it. I believe this is what God desires from us: not rigid perfection, but pliability. He seeks a heart that is readily molded, a spirit tender enough to sense His whisper, and a life that will bend when He beckons. Yes, God expects His children to be willing to move, willing to change, willing to go wherever He leads, even into uncomfortable places.

That is godly beauty.

Jesus offered the ultimate example. In Luke 22:27, Jesus says, "For who is greater, the one who is at the table or the one who serves? Is it not the one who is at the table? But I am among you as one who serves." And don't forget Matthew 20:28: "Just as the Son of Man did not come to be served, but to serve, and to give his life as a ransom for many."

The prophet Isaiah displayed a willing and submissive heart when he responded, "Here am I. Send me!" (Isaiah 6:8).

Of course, Scripture also shows us those who resisted. Jonah ran from God's call and ended up being swallowed by a great fish (Jonah 1:3, 17). Yet when he finally yielded, his reluctant obedience led to the repentance of an entire city (Jonah 3:3-9). David once grasped for what was forbidden, choosing Bathsheba over God's command, and it led to devastating sin (2 Samuel 11). But when he bent in repentance, God restored him and used him as Israel's greatest king and the psalmist whose words still guide us in worship today (Psalm 51).

The stories of Jonah and David remind us that God's purpose prevails when we finally yield to His hands. Their lives show us that failure does not disqualify us-resistance does not end our story. What matters is whether we allow ourselves to be reshaped. In God's hands, even the broken and unwilling can become vessels of His glory.

Setting aside personal preference for obedience requires surrender. But don't confuse surrender with passivity. Surrender is active-it requires courage, especially in the face of discomfort.

If I am being honest, I haven't always yielded to the shaping process. I am not a fan of pain, and when God starts cutting away at habits or traits that I've grown to love, it hurts! I also tend to throw up all my defenses when God calls me out of my comfort zone. I prefer to stay safe and warm inside my self-made cocoon.

I remember years ago sitting in church listening to a sermon about evangelism-not the global, Billy Graham type, but the everyday, average person kind. In passing, the pastor said, "If the Spirit prompts you to speak, don't silence Him with your comfort."

I felt a Holy Spirit tickle, a quiver in the pit of my stomach. I knew those words were meant for me. You know what I'm talking about. When a word or phrase hits you in a way you can't ignore. When the verse just won't leave you alone, and you know it's a prompt from God.

I thought of times I had silenced the Spirit before, and one moment especially echoed in my heart. It was a calm Thursday afternoon. I had popped into a diner for a quick lunch. It was nothing fancy, just a tiny building tucked neatly off the main street. A handful of customers ate in silence. I always enjoyed the slow, still atmosphere where I could hear my own thoughts. Over the years, I had spent many hours in a corner booth preparing for a Sunday School or discipleship class. The peaceful setting was perfect for hearing the Holy Spirit.

It was the waitress who caught my attention on this particular day. She looked... tired. Not the kind you only see in the eyes, but the kind that permeates the entire body. Her bearing spoke of a burden far heavier than mere physical tiredness. The moment she came to fill my glass, I felt it. That unmistakable stirring.

"Ask her if she's okay." A gentle prodding, almost a whisper that sank like a stone in the back of my mind. "Ask. Not to pry. Not to fix. Just to see her. Just to care."

I didn't.

Instead, I smiled, too quickly, and thanked her. Looking away, I let the moment pass. And as I sat there in that booth stirring soup that had lost its taste, a deep heaviness settled in my heart. I had heard His voice. I had felt His presence. Yet, I had chosen silence.

Why? Out of fear. Fear of being misunderstood. Fear of overstepping bounds. Fear of awkwardness. Or perhaps, more deeply, fear of not knowing what to do if she truly opened up. I told myself it wasn't the right time. Maybe someone else would ask her. Maybe she didn't want to be put on the spot.

But I knew. God had given me an opportunity, and I had dismissed it because it was not presented in a comfortable package. That day, I came to a very sobering realization: my faith depended upon my preferences, not upon His will. I cared more about politeness than obedience. I was more afraid of discomfort than I was eager to be of use.

I remembered the words of Isaiah 64:8: "Yet you, LORD, are our Father. We are the clay; you are the potter; we are all the work of your hand."

The verse had been an encouragement in the past, but on this day, it brought only rebuke. Clay doesn't set its own limits or resist the Potter's hand. Clay yields. It surrenders to the shaping because it believes that the Potter sees something greater than the lump of earth from which it began. Through the yielding nature of that ribbon, God was inviting me to be soft again. Not passive, but pliable. He was asking me to stop resisting and start responding. That moment in the diner stayed with me, not as a source of guilt, but as a lesson: God doesn't ask for great things from us-He simply asks for a willing, moldable heart.

Sometimes, the most sacred thing we can offer is not a sermon or Scripture but mere availability. A heart saying, "Lord, shape me, bend me, use me."

In my pastor's sermon just yesterday, he said, "When God calls, you don't negotiate. You say yes."

Did he know that I was writing on this very topic? No. Was God using those words to gently sculpt my heart and my will? Most certainly. You see, I, too, need reminders.

The more I thought about the missed moment in the diner, the more clearly I saw myself. I was comfortable hearing from God. And I readily obeyed... as long as it didn't cost me anything or require me to take a risk. I didn't want to feel uncomfortable or vulnerable; I didn't want to seem foolish or step into the unknown. My resistance to God wasn't due to spiritual blindness, but the result of spiritual hard-heartedness. It was an attitude that placed my will ahead of God's. That truth was both hurtful and humbling.

What I learned that day was this: yielding isn't something

you can turn on and off at your convenience. The truth is, most surrender comes clothed in some level of discomfort. It challenges you to step out of your routine and into the unknown. This kind of obedience shapes your character. But so does resistance, which seldom hurts less.

When my stepfather passed away in August of 2019, my sister agreed to stay with Mom for a time. She was frail, and we didn't want her to be alone. In early December, I felt God urging me to go and relieve my sister. I gave God several reasons why I couldn't go. Both my husband and I were needed to manage our growing business; if I left, we would surely fall behind. I watched my grandchildren when my daughter and son-in-law's work schedules conflicted. And finally, I left home at eighteen to escape the chaos of our dysfunctional family. Even forty years later, I had no desire to return for any length of time. Surely, God would understand! But He didn't let up, and I reluctantly gave in.

After much prayer, God and I determined that I would leave for Mom's on March 13, 2020, and return home on May 26-a total of 75 days!

I was hesitant, but God graciously revealed His sovereignty before I even arrived. While I was driving, the President declared a national emergency due to the COVID-19 pandemic and ordered the closure of all non-essential businesses. God knew what He was doing after all; He knew there would be no business to worry about!

His hand didn't stop there. During our time together, Mom

and I played cards and watched game shows. I helped with household chores and online grocery orders, and by the end of my stay, the uneasiness that typically defined our visits faded. Mom seemed to trust my motives more than she had in the past, and I began to see her not as the one who had wounded me but as someone who also had been wounded. She, too, was a woman in need of love and mercy.

When I returned home, the change between us lingered. For the next ten months, Mom and I spoke nearly every day, and the steady rhythm of our conversations became a gift I hadn't known I needed. That's why I grew concerned when she didn't answer the phone or return my calls. After requesting a wellness check from the local police department, I received the news I never wanted to hear: they found Mom in her bed. She was gone.

When the initial shock faded, I realized that God hadn't sent me to stay with Mom as a punishment. Rather, out of His great love and mercy, He provided an opportunity for healing. If I had disobeyed and stayed in my comfort zone, we both would have missed God's blessings. Had I not spent that time with Mom, her distrust of me would have remained, and I might still harbor disappointment, bitterness, and anger toward her. But because I yielded to God, He healed two hearts.

Through my obedience, God bent the ribbon of my soul. He twisted it in a way I had not imagined, folded it in a season I would have chosen to avoid, and something beautiful emerged. I realized that obedience does not necessarily result in fireworks. At times, it leads to peace. At times, the reward is not trophies or visible progress, but the gentle restoration of a tired relationship. Or it is simply the pure joy of knowing that you heard God and said yes. That in itself is a great reward. Because yielding does not diminish you, it shapes you. Your pliability moves your faith to action. When you let go of your resistance and submit to the hands of the Potter, He reveals a version of you that you never imagined could be. Softer. Braver. Freer.

1 Corinthians 9:22-23 says this: "I have become all things to all people so that by all possible means I might save some. I do all this for the sake of the gospel."

Yielding is not relinquishing yourself; rather, it is becoming available. It's letting go of your need for control long enough for God to create a better story than the one you had written. There was a time when I believed that strength was defined by certainty, boundaries, and plans; however, God has shown me that genuine strength is often found in surrender, in letting Him coax you out of your comfort zone and into places you would never choose by yourself. For it is in those very places that healing, purpose, and grace meet.

Submission is not a sign of weakness. On the contrary, it signifies willingness, flexibility, and availability. Just like the ribbon, our hearts are to be pliable and responsive to His touch. I still regret not speaking to the waitress in the diner. But God, in His kindness, offers new chances. New moments. New prompts.

I have learned to say yes more quickly since then. To lean into awkward. To trust that if He opens a door, He will walk through it with me. More importantly, I have learned that the beauty of a life surrendered is not in flawlessness, but in the willingness to obey when God calls.

May your heart be like a ribbon-soft, submissive, willing, and obedient. May He shape you into the beauty of the vessel you were meant to be.

Reflection

"Yet you, LORD, are our Father. We are the clay, you are the potter; we are all the work of your hand."

(Isaiah 64:8)

"I have become all things to all people so that by all possible means I might save some. I do all this for the sake of the gospel."

(1Corinthians 9:22-23)

Q: What do these verses reveal about God's role as the potter and your role as clay in His hands?

_____

_____

_____

(Please continue in your own journal!)

Q: In what areas of your life might God be reshaping you so that others can see the gospel more clearly through you?

_____

_____

_____

(Please continue in your own journal!)

Q: How would your daily choices and relationships change if you fully surrendered to God's shaping hand, allowing Him to use you to reach others for Christ?

_____

_____

_____

(Please continue in your own journal!)

Q: How does Paul's willingness to become "all things to all people" show what it looks like to be shaped by God for His purposes?

_____

_____

_____

(Please continue in your own journal!)

Prayer

Lord,

You are the Potter and I am the clay. I am the work of Your hands. Take my selfish thoughts and desires and replace them with a willing spirit. Mold me into a vessel that You can use to accomplish Your purpose in my life. Help me to surrender to You always.

In the powerful name of Jesus, Amen.

Chapter Seven

Frayed, but Favored

Imperfection Does NOT Disqualify You

Christians often repeat this quote: "You don't have to be perfect, just present." I can personally vouch for the truth of that statement. During a Sunday sermon some twenty-five years ago, I thought, *I wish I had a job that required me to study the Bible.* Though I shared that thought with no one, I was asked several weeks later to take over the Sunday School class my husband and I attended. It was an answer to my prayer, but I was far from qualified. I had never taught before and could never compete with the wisdom of the man I would replace.

Despite my inadequacy, I accepted the challenge. I'm sure class members would confirm that I was less than perfect, but I was willing and available. Even with my mistakes, the next twenty-three years presented learning opportunities that would not have been possible if I had waited for just the right qualifications. God doesn't disqualify us because of imperfection or weakness. Instead, He uses our willingness to overcome our weakness and our presence to defeat our imperfection.

I recalled that lesson as I lifted the ribbon to open my Bible. The red glinted quietly, the gold shimmered with promise, but the edges were what drew me in today. Frayed. Undone.

Wearing thin where time had caught them and fingers had held on. I paused to rub one corner with my thumb. The strand of gold that once held red threads in place now stood separate, leaving abandoned fabric to fall aimlessly with no form or purpose. Golden beads that once formed a single straight line now randomly rose and fell.

There was a time when I would have considered the ribbon worthless. I would have tossed it aside as trash in favor of something not tainted. Something perfect. But today the ribbon seemed to issue a new message, one that welcomed imperfection and hinted that weakness didn't necessarily mean worthlessness.

The battered beads and stray strands that I once considered flaws now felt more like proof-proof that this ribbon had been touched, handled, knotted and unknotted, folded into meaning, and slid through moments in time. I could picture it hanging proudly in places where stories were shared, prayers were whispered, and tears fell. It had been present for its calling. And through all of its use, the ribbon had survived. It had submitted to the twisting and reshaping, over and over again, and proudly served its purpose.

The marks of survival-the twisting and fraying-took nothing away from the ribbon's beauty or worth. If anything, the scars added to it.

And aren't we the same way? Don't we bear the scars of a lifetime-scars of pain, shame, abuse, and disappointment? Some wounds are uncovered, visible for all to see. We are forced to face those reminders, to deal with them every day. But it is the hidden hurt that hangs heaviest on our hearts. The pain that pierces so deep that we question our worth. We wonder if a perfect God can really use someone with scars and deficiencies.

The answer, my friend, is yes. He can and He does! With your life, just as with the ribbon, it is in the fray that the real story is revealed.

When God chooses to use you, it is not the polished, unblemished parts that He reaches for first, but the worn, threadbare edges that prove you have lived, fallen, and risen again; that you have survived... by His grace.

I didn't always believe that. I spent the better part of my life convincing myself that usefulness was reserved for the flawless, that I needed to be spiritually spotless before I could serve, that I needed to memorize more Scripture, be healed from every hurt, and silence every insecurity. I imagined that God only used polished vessels, not chipped ones like me. So, I quietly accepted my disqualification and took a seat in the back row of opportunity.

But I've since learned that God is not waiting for your perfection. He is reaching out to your availability. Believe it or not, your spiritual condition is no secret to God! Those brave souls who recognize their need and unashamedly present their frayed ends to Him-it is through them that God's glory shines.

With that lesson behind me, what did I do when asked to

lead a Bible study? I did what any perfectly imperfect person would do. I panicked. Not just a minor flutter of nerves but full-blown, stomach-twisting, are-they-serious panic. I felt no joy or excitement, and certainly no sense of calling or confidence. No, I felt fear, dread, and doubt that asked, "Who am I to lead anyone?"

In my mind, a slideshow instantly began playing every failure I had ever hidden from the public eye. I witnessed again every harsh word uttered in frustration; every season when I wandered from God; every instance where fear reigned and faith shrank. I even tried to redirect the teaching task, like a misaddressed letter, but the Spirit kept returning it to me-sealed with grace.

I thought, *I haven't prayed enough; I'm not smart enough; I'm just not enough. I'm not qualified. Period.*

There was no doubt about it; this had to be a mistake. So, I picked up the phone and called a dear friend, hoping she would validate my reluctance so that I could bow out with a clear conscience.

"I feel like the ribbon on the bottom of the box," I finally spoke quietly, as if I were reporting a crime, "flawed and unworthy."

She did not rush to respond. Instead, there was a void, a holy silence that seemed to carry a wisdom all its own. And then my friend uttered something profound: "Pam... perhaps that's the kind of ribbon God wants to use."

This time, I was silent as her words echoed over and over in my mind. As the message sank in, a new perspective began to form.

Could it be that God wasn't looking for a polished individual but one who was present? Someone who understood what it meant to be frayed but faithful at the same time?

I wrestled with that thought for days. I prayed. I cried. I doubted. I reminded God of all the other people who were more qualified, more eloquent-more everything-than me.

But even in my pleading, I began to see the truth of how God chooses. He doesn't review resumes and accolades in search of spotless track records. God reads our hearts; He measures our willingness, and He honors our availability.

The words of 1 Corinthians 1:26-27 flooded my mind:

> Brothers and sisters, think of what you were when you were called. Not many of you were wise by human standards; not many were influential; not many were of noble birth. But God chose the foolish things of the world to shame the wise; God chose the weak things of the world to shame the strong.

It was becoming clear. God does not reject the weak; He embraces them. He does not avoid the broken. He calls them. He does not shy away from the fray; He welcomes it because, within the fraying threads and broken pieces, His glory is most vividly seen.

Take David, for example. Though just a boy, he was willing to face the Philistine giant Goliath when no Israelite soldier would. He was young and small, weak compared to Goliath, but David was willing to offer what he had to serve his God. And we all know how that turned out. God used David's willingness to defeat Goliath and bring victory to the Israelites.

Then there was Peter. He was impulsive, hot-tempered, and always speaking before thinking. But even before Peter's denial, Jesus spoke these words to him:

> And I tell you that you are Peter, and on this rock I will build my church, and the gates of Hades will not overcome it. I will give you the keys of the kingdom of heaven; whatever you bind on earth will be bound in heaven, and whatever you loose on earth will be loosed in heaven. (Matthew 16:18-19)

Jesus knew Peter's flaws, but He also knew his heart.

And what about the woman at the well? (John 4:7-42) Her story will always move me. Married and divorced five times, she had a reputation that sent whispers rippling through her village. But, despite her sin and reputation, Jesus chose her. He offered her living water. And then, because she was willing, Jesus used this scorned woman to bring the Good News to the very people who had already judged and disqualified her. What a picture of grace!

Why does God call the flawed and the unqualified? Because no one this side of heaven is perfect. Ecclesiastes 7:20 tells us: "Indeed, there is no one on earth who is righteous, no one who does what is right and never sins."

Instead, God takes our imperfections and transforms them into a testimony. Rahab was a prostitute living in Jericho when the twelve Israelite spies came to assess the land. She recognized that the Almighty God was with these men and agreed to help them. In return, she and her family were spared and became part of the nation of Israel. Through marriage, Rahab became an ancestor of King David and is listed in the genealogy of Jesus (Joshua 2; Joshua 6:22-25; Matthew 1:5)!

So when you are tempted to think that your messiness repels God, offends His holiness, or disqualifies you because of your broken places, remember the God of David, Peter, and the woman at the well. Remember that Jesus healed lepers, dined with outcasts, and spoke with Samaritans. There is nothing you can bring to Him that will push Him away.

Quite the contrary. Your mess pulls Him nearer. Psalm 34:18 gently assures us: "The LORD is close to the brokenhearted and saves those who are crushed in spirit." That verse illuminates the divine tenderness of a Savior who does not stand apart but runs toward your pain. He leans in when others step back. He is not ashamed of your brokenness; He does His best work there.

Because in the midst of brokenness, there is beauty.

I see that ribbon now, its edges worn, its threads broken and brittle in places, and I see no damage. I see proof. I see life.

Not just wear, but witness. Those fibers tell the story of being folded and refolded; tugged by trials, kissed by tears, but still here.

And so are you. You have been hurt. You have been devastated by disappointment. You've weathered storms you never saw coming; you've carried invisible burdens. But you are still here.

Those scars and rough edges? They are not blemishes. They are badges of honor that prove grace held you when strength ran out. They say God was faithful while you were falling apart.

The words of Isaiah 40:29 ring so true: "He gives strength to the weary and increases the power of the weak."

Now let's return to the Bible study I agreed to lead and a memory that is etched in my mind like an old photograph. I stood trembling before the group. All were older and much wiser than I was. These disciples sat ready with Bibles open, hearts hungry, and eyes fixed on me. My hands shook. My legs nearly gave way. My voice quivered. Then something settled over me: peace. Not the kind that comes with experience and self-confidence. I had neither. It was the peace that flows from what Isaiah spoke of-strength given to the weary, power poured into the weak. It was confidence not in myself, but in the One who called me despite my weakness-the One who said, "I see your brokenness and your flaws and I still choose you."

Now, this ribbon with its frayed edges speaks softly to my soul: "God doesn't need perfect; He just needs present."

So, if you are reading this with a quiet ache in your chest, thinking you are too flawed to matter, hear me loud and clear: you are not too far gone. You are not too broken. You are not too small. You are exactly the type of person God likes to use. Let your ribbon be seen. Don't hide the fray. Don't tuck your story away as if it doesn't count in His kingdom. That edge worn by struggle is also touched by glory.

Do you recall the story of the man blind from birth? The disciples asked Jesus the reason for his blindness. His response says it all: "Neither this man nor his parents sinned," said Jesus, "but this happened so that the works of God might be displayed in him" (John 9:3).

Jesus' words in John 9 remind us that imperfection and suffering are not punishments, nor are they disqualifications from God's love or His purposes. Instead, they can become the very stage where His glory is displayed. The man born blind was not defined by what he lacked, but by what God would reveal through him. That truth still holds today. Nick Vujicic and Joni Eareckson Tada are living testimonies of this reality-lives that, though marked by limitation, shine with the brilliance of God's work.

Nick Vujicic was born without arms and legs-an imperfection the world might see as disqualifying. But God has used his life to reach millions. Like the ribbon others might have discarded, Nick's surrendered life has been lifted up and trimmed with gold, a testimony that our limitations don't lessen our worth. Instead, they highlight the power of God who delights in using what seems weak to display His strength.

Joni Eareckson Tada's accident left her paralyzed, but it did not disqualify her from God's work. In fact, her surrender through imperfection has revealed a deeper beauty. For decades, she has reminded the world that God doesn't need perfection to use us-He needs willingness. What looked like limitation became her platform to display His glory.

Nick and Joni's stories-and countless others-prove that your imperfections do not disqualify you from God's purposes. Instead, they become the very canvas where His beauty is displayed. Jesus' words in John 9:3 echo through their testimonies and through my own life as well. This verse has brought me great comfort over the years. It didn't erase the sadness of a friend's sickness or the pain of watching a family member suffer. But it reminded me that suffering never escapes God's notice. He sees it, and He can use even the hardest circumstances to reveal His glory. After all, it is not the absence of weakness that makes you useful, but the presence of a God who delights in showing His power through imperfect people.

Remember, you are not frayed but favored. God has never shunned your ragged edges-He welcomes them. Because in your weakness, His glory shines the brightest.

Reflection

*"But God chose the foolish things of the world to shame the wise;
God chose the weak things of the world to shame the strong."*

(1 Corinthians 1:27)

*"Not that we are competent in ourselves to claim anything for
ourselves, but our competence comes from God."*

(2 Corinthians 3:5)

**Q: What do these verses reveal about God's way of
working through weakness rather than human strength?**

_____

_____

_____

(Please continue in your own journal!)

**Q: How does knowing that your competence comes
from God change the way you see your own limitations?**

_____

_____

_____

(Please continue in your own journal!)

Q: Where in your life do you tend to rely on your own wisdom or strength instead of God's power?

_____

_____

_____

(Please continue in your own journal!)

Q: How might embracing God's strength in your weakness free you to live with greater humility, boldness, and trust in His calling on your life?

_____

_____

_____

(Please continue in your own journal!)

Prayer

Father, thank You that my worth and competence come not from myself but from You. Teach me to see my weakness as an opportunity for Your power to be displayed. Help me to rely less on my own strength and more on Your Spirit, so that my life points others to You.

In the powerful name of Jesus, Amen.

Chapter Eight

Light Through the Ribbon

God Can Always Be Found

Grief does not announce itself. Not a word or a courtesy call before it barges in, noisy, brutal, and certainly uninvited, splintering whatever peace you thought you had. In November of 2020, grief did not just come into my life: it kicked the door down, shattered the frame into pieces, and left my soul in ruins.

That was when I lost my eldest grandson. A mere thirteen years old. *Thirteen.* He had overcome many physical obstacles in his young life. Though others would certainly arise, he had a future, a potential still to be fulfilled. But just like that, he was gone. No warnings. No explanation. Just gone.

No blueprint exists for that type of loss. No instruction manual details how a grandmother goes about burying her grandson. There simply are no words capable of capturing that kind of sorrow. Logic isn't sharp enough to carve answers out of silence. No well-intentioned platitudes, no casseroles, no comforting Scriptures-even those I had quoted a thousand times before-could dull the sound my heart made when it split apart.

I was devastated. But beyond that, I was angry. Fiercely.

Unapologetically. Unreasonably angry. Angry at a God I had walked with, wept with, trusted, worshipped, and served for decades. Angry that this happened to someone so innocent. The kind of anger that doesn't just flare and fade but simmers, hot and heavy, filling every breath. I knew God was good. I had told others He was good, encouraged them with Scripture, and even stood in front of crowds giving testimonies of His faithfulness. But as I stared into the space vacated by my grandson, those words felt hollow, like echoes from another lifetime. My heart was split wide open, my theology colliding with my grief. I found it impossible to reconcile my understanding of God with the depth of my heartbreak. It was more than sorrow-it was betrayal. Betrayal by the very One I had trusted most, the One who promised to answer prayer and be near to the brokenhearted. And in that silence, I felt abandoned.

In the days that followed, I couldn't bear to pray. The words would not come; they were locked somewhere deep inside, buried under the rubble of my pain. And even if they had surfaced, I wouldn't have spoken them. My heart lay wide open and bleeding, raw and exposed, and I wanted God out of the mess I believed He had created.

So, I shut Him out. I stopped going to church, too wounded to endure the sight of people lifting their hands in worship when mine felt paralyzed with grief. I turned the worship music off-the same songs that once brought comfort now felt like salt in a wound. I closed my Bible, unable to face the promises that seemed broken, hollow, and cruel. Even saying His name felt foreign, offensive, like poison on my tongue. All I could taste was a sharp bitterness that was not easily washed away.

Deep inside, beneath the heaviness, I knew I still needed Him. The faith that had steadied me for so many years whispered that He was still my refuge, still my only real shelter. But knowing it and trusting it were two different things. Trusting Him again would mean opening my heart to vulnerability. It would mean letting the same hands that allowed this heartbreak be the ones to hold me. And I couldn't do that. Not anymore. Not when trusting Him had led me straight into this wilderness of unanswered questions and unbearable grief.

So, I did what many do in their pain-I just shut down. It felt easier to numb myself than to risk feeling the sharp edges of loss again. I built walls around my heart and called it survival, though deep down I knew it was more like a prison. Those walls were thick, heavy, impenetrable. They kept out the ache, but they also kept out the light.

I closed my ears to the gentle urging of the Holy Spirit, the same voice that had always felt like home. Now even that familiar whisper seemed intrusive, unwanted. I pushed away the words of Scripture, words that once felt alive and breathing, pulsing with hope, but now lay flat and cold on the page. The Bible sat unopened, collecting dust like an old relic from a life I wasn't sure I believed in anymore.

I convinced myself that silence was safer than surrender, that distance was safety. Yet the quiet was deafening. Prayers that once rose easily from my lips now sank unspoken, swallowed by sorrow. The silence was heavy, suffocating, yet I told myself it was strength. In truth, it was fear. Fear of being wounded again. Fear that if I reached for God, He might turn away. Fear that if I trusted, the pain would only cut deeper.

But God didn't leave me or abandon me. He simply was not offended enough to storm off. He did not scold me for my doubts or cause me additional pain. He did not tell me to get my act together and move on. No, He stayed. Silent. Patient. Faithful.

God is true to His word: "He will never leave you nor forsake you" (Deuteronomy 31:6).

Like a soft glow of light behind a sheer ribbon, His presence-so dim it was nearly imperceptible-was somehow there. Translucent. Heavenly. Steady. Refusing to fade away completely, even when everything within me tried to shut Him out. Because this is who God is.

He does not run when faith falters; He is Immanuel-God with us-who stands waiting at the edge of our pain until we are ready to see Him again. And as I became ready, there was no drama. No rolled thunder. No lightning bolts. No angelic chorus. Not one prophetic dream to explain it all. No cutting-edge miraculous moment that simply washed away my grief with a strong, tide-like current. Just a steady presence slowly inching its way back into my heart.

An unexplainable companionship quietly remained. A divine thread connecting heaven and my broken heart. It was subtle. Soft. Like the outline of a shadow in the fog, dim at first, almost invisible, but undeniably there if I looked long enough.

That's how I remember God in that season. Not absent. Not punishing. Just... veiled. Hidden behind the haze of my pain. Gentle in His approach. Patient in His presence. Translucent. How strange that sometimes the most perfect miracles are the most subtle and quiet ways in which God remains with us. I couldn't see Him distinctly. I couldn't feel His comfort like I used to. But still, my soul knew: He hadn't left me. He had just silenced Himself in the volume of my sorrow.

Then, one night, with no planning or ceremony, I whispered the smallest prayer I could muster. "I don't know what to say... but I'm here."

That was it. Nine words. Not polished. Not poetic. No Scriptures. No "thank you." Just a bruised offering by a woman who was simply too tired to pretend any longer.

My voice trembled, thin and hesitant, as the words left my lips, and I half expected nothing in return. That moment felt fragile, like the first conversation with a friend after a painful argument. I was unsure how to begin yet desperate to release what I had held inside.

Then came the response. It was not empty silence, but stillness. A sacred stillness. The kind that does not wail, but rests like the glow of a lamp in the window, guiding you back to the certainty that you are not alone.

That prayer-so naked and frazzled-was not closure but a

commencement. It was an inner shift so subtle I may have missed it. It was not dramatic, nor did it occur all at once. It was progressive, like mounds of ice and snow that steadily thaw after a long winter.

That heartfelt yet somewhat hollow cry somehow warmed my heart, and my defensiveness toward God began to melt away. Little by little, feelings of betrayal were replaced by an innate need for prayer. Honest prayer. Not to impress Him or recite half-hearted truths. I merely wanted to be near Him, to be in His presence. Somehow, that was all I needed.

With that quiet, nearly imperceptible turn, the Holy Spirit began to heal the very wound I had so carefully hidden. Rather than ripping off the bandage, He sat beside me, soothed me, and began to stitch up the wounds left by sorrow.

I returned to the Scriptures, though more for relief than for study. And as I read, God was there:

> Where can I go from your Spirit? Where can I flee from your presence? If I go up to the heavens, you are there; if I make my bed in the depths, you are there. If I rise on the wings of the dawn, if I settle on the far side of the sea, even there your hand will guide me, your right hand will hold me fast (Psalm 139:7-10).

I had read the verses before. Quoted them. Underlined and highlighted them in my Bible. But at this moment, they were more than theological; they were air in my lungs as I lay drowning in the depths. I had sunk so low in sorrow that I no longer remembered what it was to look up. And yet, there He was. Not with answers. Not with explanations. But with His presence. And that, as it turns out, is more powerful than understanding. Presence does not have to solve anything-it simply sticks around. And the God I accused of abandoning me had never moved. He just encased everything in silence so that He could walk me through my pain. His hold was firm because He had never let go of me.

I eventually returned to church. Not out of any feeling of courage. Not because the haze had lifted or answers had been found. I didn't enter with a faith freshly restored or with a heart full of hallelujahs; I came in with a limp. A soul still aching from so much wrestling. I came in quietly, heavy, scarred, and yet willing. And sometimes, willingness is enough.

I didn't know what I would face. Would the songs rekindle my sorrow? Would the prayers pierce through my pain, or would they hold no meaning? Would I feel out of place in a place I once called home?

Yet when I stepped across that threshold, I felt no judgment, no pressure to perform. There were no platitudes thrust upon me, and I was not required to explain my absence. Instead, I felt... held. Not by the people, though they were kind. Not by the music, though it was beautiful. I was held by His presence.

That's the business of God. He doesn't wait until the wounds are healed to welcome you home. He runs straight toward the wound-the mess, the blood, the sorrow-and whispers, "I'm still here."

He is the light shining through the ribbon. Dim, perhaps, to your grieving eyes. Subtle. Easy to miss when pain clouds your view. But never absent. Never failing.

I had always thought God's presence would burst into a room, that I would know it by signs and wonders, that it would be unmistakable. Now I know the truth: His presence is often faint. Almost translucent. Like sunlight trying to push through clouds in a stormy sky or perhaps through a folded ribbon hanging gracefully in a window. That's what His presence felt like in that season. Not loud. Not obvious. But faithful. Always faithful.

Jeremiah 29:13 reads: "You will seek me and find me when you seek me with all your heart." For many years, I believed seeking God with all my heart meant piously presenting a clean offering to Him. Pure motives. Immutable hope. Hands up in unwavering faith.

But it doesn't have to look that way. Sometimes, seeking Him with all your heart means dragging your broken self to the pew and just showing up. Sometimes, it's a prayer murmured between clenched teeth and wet cheeks while clinging to the slimmest thread of belief that He is still good when life has been anything but. Sometimes, it sounds more like giving up than a song.

And in that, He is glorified. He honors the wounded who

walk in late and sit in the back. He blesses the silent tears, the reluctant hallelujahs, the prayers mired in agony that begin with, "I don't know if You're listening…" and conclude with, "But I really need You."

It's clear now when I look back: I was not forsaken. God was just blurred out of focus by a weighty grief and vision that adapted to the dark and forgot what light was. But God? He never moved. He did not turn His face away. He did not retreat. It was as if He drew a sheer, holy veil between us. Not to hide Himself from me, but to protect me. He knew what I couldn't yet see-that I wasn't ready for brilliance. I needed subtle light. Gentle light. The kind that meets you where you are, not where you think you should be.

The ribbon that once glimmered with certainty now sat dulled under the shadow of loss. But it never disappeared. It stayed. It swayed in stillness, catching whatever light it could, quietly waiting for me to see again. And when my eyes adjusted and my heart cracked open just a sliver-it came into view.

The ribbon. Faint. Consistent. Beautiful. Not because it had changed, but because I had.

To anyone sitting in that darkness right now, know this: He's still there. Even when the silence is deafening. Even when your heart is too shattered to lift a prayer. Even when every attempt to feel His presence ends in emptiness. He hasn't left you. He hasn't given up on you. He's that soft light threading through your sorrow, that steady hand beneath your collapse, the whisper in the dark reminding you: you are not alone. He is the light reaching through the ribbon. Gentle, unwavering, present. And He's not letting go.

Not now. Not ever.

Reflection

"I love those who love me, and those who seek me find me."

(Proverbs 8:17)

"And surely I am with you always, to the very end of the age."

(Matthew 28:20)

Q: What do these verses teach us about God's promise to be present with those who seek Him?

_____

_____

_____

(Please continue in your own journal!)

Q: How does the assurance of God's nearness change the way you approach seasons of doubt, fear, or loneliness?

_____

_____

_____

(Please continue in your own journal!)

Q: In what ways can you more intentionally seek God's presence in your daily life and decisions?

_____

_____

_____

(Please continue in your own journal!)

Q: How might living with the constant awareness that God is both findable and always with you reshape your trust, your worship, and your sense of purpose?

_____

_____

_____

(Please continue in your own journal!)

Prayer

Merciful Father,

Thank You that You love me and promise to be with me always. Forgive me for the times that I turned from You. Help me to seek You earnestly today, in my thoughts, choices, and actions. Open my eyes to Your presence and my heart to Your love. Remind me that even when I feel distant, You are near. Teach me to walk confidently in Your guidance, trusting that Your Spirit is with me in every moment.

In Jesus' name, Amen.

Chapter Nine

Repurposed-The Call to New Seasons

God Is Never Finished With You

In 1942, Americans were asked to recycle everyday items for the war effort. Paper, rags, metal-even cooking oil-were reprocessed to serve a greater purpose. Since then, recycling has become a symbol of hope: that what seems used-up or unwanted can still be made useful again.

Evidence of this repurposing is everywhere. You see bins marked with "Recycle" at popular places like schools, city streets, and church fellowship halls. These bins are more than just containers; they are symbols of hope. Hope that even hand-me-down, unwanted items can still be used for something good, that they can serve a new and different purpose. It seems that with the right process, nearly everything can be made useful again.

In my home, aluminum, tin, and plastic are set aside, not for disposal, but for redemption. Rather than being discarded as useless, this trash is surrendered to someone who transforms it into something new and useful.

At church, for example, my Sunday School class collects plastic grocery bags, the kind most of us ball up and shove into a drawer or toss under the sink, unsure of what else to do with them.

Each week, class members bring in plastic grocery bags-the kind we usually stuff in drawers or toss away. Flattened, shredded, heated, and pressed, they're turned into sturdy park benches. I once spotted one of these benches, ordinary to the eye, yet extraordinary to me. What moved me was knowing that something flimsy and forgotten had been reshaped to carry the weight of another.

While mankind increasingly embraces the concept of reusing and repurposing, we did not invent it. God wove recycling into the very fabric of creation. Organisms like earthworms, beetles, and lichens help return nutrients to the soil by breaking down dead plants and animals. Water is constantly recycled through evaporation, condensation, and precipitation. And hermit crabs take up residence in abandoned shells. The intricate details of God's design in nature have always amazed me!

But God also reclaims and repurposes His people-you and me. He works through the broken, the lost, and even those who feel too old for service. He reshapes us, presses us into something new, and fits us perfectly into His plan. This is more than recycling; it is redemption through grace.

That truth came rushing back as I held the ribbon. Its frayed edges became a vivid reminder of that redemption-proof that what looks worn can still be made useful. The faded crimson still caught the light when the sun touched it, and though I couldn't recall whether it once wrapped a box, a bouquet, or something else, it had clearly fulfilled a purpose before.

And now? Though faded and frayed, the ribbon could still be tied, wrapped, or woven into something new. Its beauty was not confined to what it had been, but to what it could still become. In the same way, God uses us in different seasons-strong in our youth, steady in our middle years, and seasoned with wisdom in our later days. No matter how frayed the edges of our story may seem, His grace ensures we remain part of His design, always redeemable, always useful, always beautiful.

As I turned the ribbon over in my hands, I heard the still, unmistakable whisper of God: "You are not discarded. You are repurposed."

Let that sit with you for a moment. You are not thrown away. You are being transformed. You are not past your prime. You are being prepared for what is next. God doesn't waste people, and certainly not their seasons. He doesn't panic when your titles change. He doesn't see age as a barrier. He sees every life as a canvas and every season as a brushstroke.

The Bible is full of stories like this. David shows us that God develops hearts in hidden places long before public crowns. Paul reminds us that even a painful past does not disqualify us-God can redirect a persecutor into a preacher. Noah proves it's never too late to obey, answering God's call at 500 years old. Abraham teaches us that God's promises are worth the wait, even if fulfillment seems impossible.

Each of their lives tells the same story: God does not rush, nor does He discard His servants. He prepares, redirects, and repurposes. And the same is true for you.

When I look back on my life, I see season after season of repurposing. Different roles. Different callings. All stitched together by a single thread of grace.

There was the season of homeschooling. Lesson plans, lunch breaks, and library trips filled my days. I became a teacher, nurse, chef, counselor, and jailer all rolled into one. Some days, I felt the overwhelming joy and peace of carrying out my calling. On other days, I hoped and prayed everyone made it to bedtime without too many tears-mine or theirs.

In those years, I thought I was shaping my children, but in truth, God was shaping me. The frustration of teaching math and grammar became His tool for teaching me patience and dependence.

Then came the season of caring for my in-laws. Fourteen years of managing meals, medicines, and appointments, punctuated by quiet afternoons of stories and movies. It felt ordinary, even dull at times, yet God was refining me in hidden ways-teaching compassion, endurance, and the beauty of unseen service.

And when He placed my two nieces in my care, I felt stretched beyond what I thought possible. Walkers and backpacks. Doctor's visits and school projects. I didn't always serve with grace, but God was chiseling me into someone who could. His strength filled the places where mine ran out.

Now I find myself in a new season-writing, reflecting, and listening more closely for His voice. The pace is quieter, but His presence is no less real. Every stage, whether chaotic or calm, has been God's way of reshaping me for His purposes. But reshaping rarely feels gentle in the moment. It is often born out of tears, exhaustion, and prayers whispered in secret.

I'll be honest-there were days it was so hard I felt I couldn't go on. I shut the door, sat on the edge of the bathtub, and wept so quietly even I could barely hear it. I didn't want to disturb anyone. Didn't want to seem ungrateful. But I was exhausted. Not just my body-my spirit too.

There were days I wondered if I mattered at all. If anything I poured out would ever be seen or remembered. I felt invisible, as if the world kept moving while I was stuck behind, rearranging pillows, sorting medications, chasing school activities.

But those years taught me more than any classroom or pulpit ever could. Through the tears and the trials, I learned that presence outweighs performance or production. That just showing up can be ministry. Those years taught me compassion: that quiet kind of chemistry that just sits next to the other person, listening, caring, not fixing.

And through the seasons, I learned to serve with a grateful heart: to tackle endless piles of laundry with a smile; to thank

God that I was able to help with homework or make a loved one's bed. Sometimes, those are the holiest of moments.

Those seasons didn't look or feel like ministry, but they most certainly were. After all, aren't we called to train our children to follow God and to care for those who can't care for themselves? Didn't Jesus demonstrate love, kindness, mercy, and compassion?

Was I perfect? Not even close. But I was present. I said yes.

And that small *yes*, offered in weakness, became the doorway through which God revealed His strength. Even if you show up with weak faith, tired and uncertain, perhaps even quaking in your boots, He will show up in power and miraculously make your little bit enough. I once saw those seasons of homeschooling, caregiving, and nurturing as interruptions within a singular, lifelong call. I now see that they were not interruptions at all. They were the call. They weren't detours but sacred highways paved with grace and illuminated by faith. God wasn't trying to push me out of usefulness. He was moving me into it. And whenever a new season was introduced, He unveiled a new plan for my purpose.

This current season is different from the others, yet my heart is as full as it's ever been. The silence is sacred. Sitting at my computer or in a recliner with my Bible open and my journal nearby, I feel the Holy Spirit softly nudging my soul, and I know God is still using me. There is no doubt in my mind. He is using my voice. My history. My healed places. My scars. God didn't stop calling my name; He is simply using me in a different way to accomplish a different purpose.

And maybe, just maybe, that is where you find yourself as well. There is no better place to be, but know this: There is a lie that sneaks in quietly when your role changes. It is a lie that whispers, "You had your moment. You're done."

At first, it is subtle, just a passing thought. And then you feel the sting of irrelevance. If left unchallenged, that lie settles into your bones. You won't pray boldly. You won't show up anymore. You won't expect God to use you anymore.

Please let me say this from the depths of my heart: Do not fall prey to that lie. God doesn't put an expiration date on purpose. He does not retire the faithful. He does not phase you out when your season changes; He folds you in deeper. In fact, some of the best works of God are in the lives of people who think they have been cast aside.

He used Moses at eighty. He gave Sarah a son in her nineties. Dear one, the hand of God does not discard you; it redirects and repurposes you. You are not junk; you are a valuable vessel. A treasure to be discovered, dusted off, and recirculated.

In Philippians 1:6, Paul tells us: "Being confident of this, that he who began a good work in you will carry it on to completion until the day of Christ Jesus." Not until your body tires. Not until your title fades. Not until society says you've aged out of usefulness. But until *completion*. God finishes what He starts. And that includes you.

In Philippians 2:13, Paul emphasizes: "For it is God who works in you to will and to act in order to fulfill his good purpose."

It's God who works in you. Not your credentials, not your energy, not even your circumstances. As long as you have breath, you have a purpose. You are not a footnote in God's story. You are a chapter still being written. A testimony still unfolding. A vessel still pouring.

So, if you find yourself in the hallway between assignments... If your hands feel idle... If your name isn't being called anymore... Lean in. Your calling isn't over. Your usefulness hasn't expired. Your service still matters because God is not done with you. He's just using you differently. More deeply. More purposefully. Let Him. Let Him repurpose your silent times into a sacred story. Let Him recycle your painful moments into ministry.

You are not done yet, friend. You are only becoming. God will do the completing. You may need to find patience in the pause and strength in the silence, but God will finish what He began if you allow Him.

The story of Simeon illustrates this perfectly.

> Now there was a man in Jerusalem called Simeon, who was righteous and devout. He was waiting for the consolation of Israel, and the Holy Spirit was on him. It had been revealed to him by the Holy Spirit that he would not die

before he had seen the Lord's Messiah. Moved by the Spirit, he went into the temple courts. When the parents brought in the child Jesus to do for him what the custom of the Law required, Simeon took him in his arms and praised God (Luke 2:25-28).

Simeon obediently and expectantly waited for God to move. And when He did, Simeon was ready. The waiting had prepared him.

That brings me back to the ribbon. It had been packed away for years. It was frayed, faded, forgotten. But it still held shimmers of light, subtle shape, and certainly purpose. So do you.

Maybe you hid yourself from the bright lights and the action, and now wonder whether God has moved on without you. He hasn't. You may be retired from working for people, but God will never retire you from working for His Kingdom. You may have passed the baton of responsibility on to others, but you have not been passed over in His plan.

Your wisdom is wanted. Your prayers are still powerful. Your presence may be the last hope in someone's life. God is not done with you, friend. Not now, not ever.

Whatever season you are in, dust yourself off and let God make something beautiful out of it. Let Him bring His plan for you to completion.

Then, you, like Simeon, can say to God, "Sovereign Lord, as

you have promised, you may now dismiss your servant in peace" (Luke 2:29). Because nothing is ever wasted in God's hands. Especially not you.

Reflection

"There is a time for everything, and a season for every activity under the heavens."

(Ecclesiastes 3:1)

"For it is God who works in you to will and to act in order to fulfill his good purpose."

(Philippians 2:13)

Q: Describe a season in your past that you thought was an inconvenience but now recognize as God's repurposing.

_____

_____

_____

(Please continue in your own journal!)

Q: How has God used different seasons of your life to shape your character and deepen your dependence on Him?

_____

_____

_____

(Please continue in your own journal!)

Q: How could God use your present circumstances-whether joyful or painful-as a testimony to others of His faithfulness and purpose?

_____

_____

_____

(Please continue in your own journal!)

Q: How might you more fully surrender your desires and actions to align with God's timing and purpose, allowing Him to use you powerfully in this season and the ones to come?

_____

_____

_____

(Please continue in your own journal!)

Prayer

Heavenly Father,

Thank You for the opportunities to serve You and for the gifts and talents You have given me. Please continue to use me as an instrument of Your grace in every season of life. Help me to be a reflection of Your love to those around me. Grant me the strength to use my abilities to honor You. May my life be a testament to Your goodness and a blessing to others.

In Jesus' name, Amen.

Chapter Ten

Silver or Gold-Discerning the Truth

Don't Be Deceived, Be Prepared

From one angle, it looked golden: that shimmer along the edge of the ribbon caught the first light of morning, each glimmer casting a warm glow that moved like firelight across my fingers. The fabric felt delicate, almost fragile, the kind you handle carefully because you're afraid it might tear. For a fleeting moment, it gleamed with royal richness-radiant, self-assured, confident. That kind of glow makes you pause. Makes you admire it. Makes you think whatever it is you are holding is special, precious, and intended for something extraordinary.

But as I tilted the ribbon just slightly, rotating it lightly through my fingers, the light shifted. What had presented itself as golden now appeared almost silver. Not even a bright silver, but dull, tired, tarnished-as though worn down by generations of handling.

I blinked. Turned it again-no sudden change. Just shifts subtle enough to cause doubt. Is it gold, or is it not? How can I know for sure? On the surface, it was a simple question of color. In reality, it exposed something much deeper: the need for discernment, recognizing the truth in a world of lies.

I learned then that deception is tricky-subtle but not invisible. It sparkles, grabs your attention, and whispers that something so beautiful can't be wrong. But I knew better. How many times had I mistaken a dream, a thought, or an opportunity for "golden," only to watch it fade? Like the high school crush who broke my heart, or the dream job that turned into a nightmare.

The ribbon now seemed more like a mirror, reflecting every pursuit of power, approval, and purpose I had chased-every moment I chose appearance over truth. The glitter once made my heart race, captured my thoughts, and convinced me the decision was right. That is the danger of deception: it doesn't feel like rebellion; it feels right.

I looked again at the ribbon lying across my palms like a tentative question mark-soft, curved, uncertain. Its weight seemed insignificant, yet at that moment, it felt as though I held the embodiment of all my unanswered prayers and wrong turns. It curled almost in protest, as if to ask: *Why did you choose that path?*

I remembered the season when I chased what I thought was a holy shimmer-a degree in Marriage and Family Counseling. It felt right. Noble, even. Helping people. Serving families. I prayed and even asked friends to pray, and without a strong "no," I pressed ahead.

When the acceptance letter arrived, my heart leapt. The envelope itself seemed to glow with promise. Surely this was confirmation. Surely this was God's favor. Even the waiting list status couldn't dull the thrill-I chose to see it as heaven's endorsement.

But time and perspective have since shown me that I never really asked for God's direction. I only asked Him to bless my desire, and when a door cracked open, I rushed through as if it bore His seal. What I didn't understand then was that not every open door is an invitation. Some are detours. Some are distractions. And some are carefully crafted tests-not to destroy, but to reveal what's hidden in the heart.

Put simply: sometimes, what you think is a blessing is really a crossroads-a moment in which you must choose to follow the glitter or follow God. And it's at that very crossroads that deception often does its most convincing work.

Looking back, I see just how cleverly deception was dressed. It carried no red warning flags; no smoke and sulfur. Graduate school didn't feel like rebellion. No, the enemy often cloaks himself in the language of purpose, in the packaging of progress, in the quiet echo of things that almost sound like God. Almost.

Friend, Satan can divert you in directions other than evil-doing to derail you. All it takes is a slight tilt, just enough to point your compass toward achievement rather than alignment. That was my story; I pursued the degree more than God. It seemed golden. It sounded godly. But the fruit of it? Spiritual distance. Emptiness. Exhaustion. Satan didn't care how hard I worked or that I believed I was working for God because he knew I was off course.

Matthew 24:24-25 warns us of deception: "For false messiahs and false prophets will appear and perform great signs and wonders to deceive, if possible, even the elect. See, I have told you ahead of time." I used to believe that verse was for the distant future, for the end times. But deception has always existed. And it doesn't always announce itself with clanging bells and dazzling lights. Rather, deception is not easy to recognize at all, much less as evil. It usually slips in through the back door, disguised with good intentions and convincing logic.

The enemy is smooth. He seldom yells; he whispers what you long to believe-that your motives are pure, that an open door must mean God's approval, that compromise won't affect your relationship with the Father.

Sound familiar? *"You will certainly not die"* (Genesis 3:4). *"For God knows that when you eat from it your eyes will be opened, and you will be like God, knowing good and evil"* (Genesis 3:5). Satan twisted God's truth and presented sin in a way that seemed attractive. He wrapped rebellion in a pretty package and hid the cost. The temptation looked so appealing that Eve found it hard to resist.

And he does the same today. His lies still sound holy, even reasonable. He buries consequences beneath promises of happiness and fulfillment. Unless God's Word is your anchor, you will be set adrift by Satan's lies-chasing what glitters while your soul quietly starves.

I lowered my head, the shame of past failures pressing in as I looked down at the ribbon. In a whisper, I confessed, "All that glitters is not gold. Every door that opens is not from God."

And I recalled my pastor gently warning me, in love, that graduate school may pull me away from God. It was not a harsh rebuke but a tender concern that I dismissed almost immediately. I smiled, thanked him, and thought to myself, *He doesn't understand. I can do this.* I naively believed that the close relationship I had cultivated with God would not suffer if I skipped an occasional Sunday School class or worship service.

And for a season, I was right. But deception generally prefers to slowly erode rather than have everything crash down at once. It never intends to frighten you; it prefers to lull you to sleep, so that the actual change escapes your notice until it is far too late.

It began with a break from teaching Sunday School-just until I settled into a new rhythm, I told myself. But weeks slipped into months, and that "pause" became permanent. Soon, church attendance became less important. My Bible lay unopened on my nightstand. I had a paper to write, a test to prepare for, and missing a Sunday seemed harmless. My faith was strong. I would be fine. After all, God knew my heart.

But God no longer held the central place in my life, and even prayer-once a sacred conversation with my Creator-became little more than a routine. A quick "Help me" before exams, a rushed "Thanks" afterward. And all the while, I was doing good things-worthy things. Learning to help people, strengthen marriages, guide families. Yet with every course, every clinical hour, every honor, my heart grew emptier. I poured out far more than my soul received, and the slow dying inside was undeniable.

The tragedy of deceit is that it rarely takes everything at once. Instead, it bargains piece by piece. A fraction of faith here, a moment of prayer there, a sense of spiritual fullness lost along the way. Each trade seems small, hardly worth noticing, until you look back and realize how much has slipped away.

That's the hidden cost: deception never announces its price. It whispers promises of purpose, approval, and meaning, but always demands something in return. And the cost is almost always greater than the reward. I mistook pursuit for progress, achievement for anointing, busyness for closeness with God. What I didn't see was the price I paid.

It wasn't until I graduated and dove back into church activities that I realized I had lost something I didn't see slipping away: intimacy with God. The relationship that was once vibrant, tender, and alive was left weak and lifeless. The voice I had so readily recognized was silenced by static and sparkle. Prayer that had once been a dialogue between two friends was now reduced to a monologue in an empty room.

My spirit felt weary, and the moment when I had stopped walking closely with Him was unclear, yet I knew it had happened. I had followed the glitter of a degree rather than the warnings from the Holy Spirit: the wait list, the tender nudges, the quiet cautions.

But what now? Getting the degree may have been a mistake, but it was done. Surely, God would take that into consideration as I pursued my career. I ignored the warning of Psalm 127:1: "Unless the LORD builds the house, the builders labor in vain." I convinced myself that if I continued to work hard, my plan would come to pass. I was determined to build a future that God did not design.

But God didn't bless what I had birthed. He didn't leave me. He simply loved me too much to sign His name on something that was never His will in the first place. I stubbornly marched through door after door, only to find dead ends and insurmountable obstacles: promised clients that never materialized and family emergencies that demanded my time. What I had believed to be a divine calling now felt like chasing after the wind. The very thing I clung to-this plan, this shimmering dream-slipped through my fingers like sand, falling away no matter how tightly I tried to hold it.

With each closed door, delay, and unexpected obstacle, my frustration grew with both God and myself. I knew. I'd felt the restlessness in my spirit. But at the time, it was all so easy to rationalize away, to cloak with determination and the language of faith.

Now, however, the truth was glaring. I had chased the shimmer, not the Shepherd. And shimmer can never place you where only His presence can take you. I had been in love with what I thought I could become. The glamor of achievement appealed to me more than resting-or as I saw it, stagnating-in the presence of the Lord. I based my identity on *my* purpose and plans, not on *His* will and *His* presence. And in so doing, I mistook movement for meaning.

"Dear friends, do not believe every spirit, but test the spirits to see whether they are from God" (1 John 4:1). If only I had done that-tested more, listened more, waited for clarity instead of rushing with convenience. I did not realize back then the magnitude of discernment, not just in keeping myself from sin, but in maneuvering within that murky place between good and God. I didn't understand-or perhaps, accept-that something could be good and yet not in God's plan.

But God never cared about my credentials or my perfect performance. He never asked for degrees or diplomas. He only wanted a heart devoted to Him, and an ear tuned to His whisper. He wanted obedience to His will rather than fulfillment of my plans. I foolishly exchanged intimacy for education and fullness of spirit for the hope of a career. And in that process, I drifted away from the sacred communion I once had with my Father. The separation was a slow unraveling, like a thread pulled loose in a sweater-subtle but undeniable. That's how Satan steals; not in an instant, but one stitch at a time.

And the cost? Far greater than tuition and textbooks, it was the isolation that comes from being out of step with His Spirit. It was the years required to recapture the security of being cocooned in His presence. Restoring the relationship took longer than any residency or licensing program because the heart doesn't heal on a deadline.

Looking again at the ribbon in my hands, the shine that once enticed me now caused pain. Not because it was evil, but because it reminded me how easily I had been duped into chasing what glimmered. The shimmer stung, not for its beauty, but for what it represented-long nights of striving and a soul quietly emptying while I pretended it was being filled. It wasn't that I didn't love God. I did. But I loved the idea of doing something "significant" even more. And that misplaced desire was the gap the enemy slipped through.

John 10:27 says, "My sheep listen to my voice; I know them, and they follow me." I thought I belonged to the Shepherd, but I made no effort to listen, chasing instead the competing sounds of ambition, affirmation, and accomplishment. Those voices had echoed so much louder in my ear than His whisper. Because that's the way deception works. It applauds the superficial and endorses ability. But God upholds truth.

Years have passed since that chapter in my life, and I'm still cautious of anything that glimmers. I question more now. I no longer run through every open door with reckless abandon. I pause. I test. I weigh what I see against what His Word affirms-not against what I want or what others praise. Because, if I'm not careful, I could mistake a good idea for a God idea. I could call a distraction a destiny. And nothing frightens me more than making that mistake again.

This world is like the edge of that ribbon-golden one second, silver the next. The glimmers and the sparkles-they look good. They sound like the truth. They may even feel right. But only the Spirit can pierce through the veil of illusion. He alone can reveal what is true and what is right.

And that's why you must remain anchored, alert, and armed. Prepared not just for the battle that boldly shouts but for the deception that delicately whispers. Remember, you don't just need direction; you need discernment. Direction points to where you should go. But discernment decides whether you should go there at all. This is the sacred filter that allows you to hear God's whisper in a world full of noise. It's the ability to pause, to press in, and to prove every opportunity, not by your logic but by His leading.

True discernment isn't born in the chaos of activity. It's built in a quiet place where it's just you and God, where ambition is laid down, where minds are calmed. Where the noise fades and His voice becomes unmistakable. When you've wrapped yourself in the Word long enough, any distortion of it is jarring to you-like hearing your favorite song played in the wrong key. That is when you know you have an anchor. Because options that seem right will always be available, some choices will always look noble. Voices that sound like God will always be there, but they are only empty echoes.

That anchor matters because deception is subtle. That's why Scripture warns us with urgency, reminding us that the enemy doesn't always come with force but with quiet persistence. "Be alert and of sober mind. Your enemy the devil prowls around like a roaring lion looking for someone to devour" (1 Peter 5:8).

Take Peter's warning to heart because you may not see Satan coming. He rarely storms the gates but waits until you leave the latch unlocked. He is subtle. But so is compromise. You will not find yourself in a sudden, grand descent. No, it begins with one unchecked motive. One "harmless" decision. One skipped Sunday. One postponed prayer. One calling quietly ignored.

Discernment sharpens your eyes to see the enemy's disguises, but it also steadies your heart to resist what merely glitters. That's why Paul's words ring so true: "Set your minds on things above, not on earthly things" (Colossians 3:2). That verse doesn't just challenge me; it compels me to stay still. It reminds me to resist sin in its obvious forms, but also the glittering alternatives: the good-but-not-God things; the distractions that sound holy but are hollow at the core.

My friend, listen to me: Not everything that shines is divine. Not every invitation is a commission. Not every open door is from the hand of God. Not every yearning in your heart comes from heaven. Deception dazzles and derails. That is why you must be prepared.

So then, how do you prepare? By training every part of yourself-your eyes, your ears, and your heart-to recognize what is real and reject what only sparkles and shines. First, train your eyes to see through the glitter-the polish, performance, cheers, and endorsements-to the emptiness it hides. Search for the truth, not the shine.

Then, train your ears to recognize His voice. Listen not simply to His words but also His tone, His patterns, and His pauses. Hear the ways He affirms, the ways He convicts, and the ways He recalls you from your wanderings. The Spirit does not confuse. He clarifies. The more you listen to His voice, the easier it will be to recognize the voice of the enemy.

Finally, train your heart to wait. "Be still before the LORD and wait patiently for him" (Psalm 37:7). Don't make the same mistake I did. Don't chase your plans; seek His. Consider the cost before making that first compromise, because truthfully, waiting may bruise pride, but deception scars the soul.

In the end, discernment is not about suspicion but about surrender-learning to trust the Spirit more than your senses and God's timing more than your own ambition. The ribbon may shimmer with golden edges, but only His hand reveals whether it is a gift to embrace or a glittering snare to resist. Train your eyes, your ears, and your heart, and you will find that even in a world of dazzling illusions, His voice remains steady, His presence constant, and His path unmistakably sure.

Reflection

"But solid food is for the mature, who by constant use have trained themselves to distinguish good from evil."
(Hebrews 5:14)

"Dear friends, do not believe every spirit, but test the spirits to see whether they are from God."
(1 John 4:1)

Q: When have you pursued something that looked "golden" but wasn't from God? What was the outcome?

_____

_____

_____

(Please continue in your own journal!)

Q: How do you test new ideas or influences to see if they align with God's truth?

_____

_____

_____

_____

Q: What helps you recognize the Shepherd's voice in your daily life, and what distractions make it harder to hear Him?

_____

_____

_____

(Please continue in your own journal!)

Q. How can you cultivate spiritual discernment? What practices or Scriptures can help you test what you see and hear?

_____

_____

_____

(Please continue in your own journal!)

Prayer

Father God,

Evil and deception are all around, and it is easy to believe the world's lies. Help me to discern Your voice above the noise; to seek You and not a shimmer. Help me to test every thought, influence, and teaching against Your truth.

Quiet the noise around me so I can hear Your voice clearly, and keep me alert to the enemy's schemes. May my life reflect trust, obedience, and a heart anchored in You.

In Jesus' name, Amen.

Chapter Eleven

Don't Put God in a Box

Awakening to His Presence

There was a time when I believed life was something that happened to me, rather than a journey I could shape, influence, or direct. It felt like I'd been placed onto a river with no oars, no maps, and no option of even suggesting where the current would carry me. I learned early that dreams were unattainable, expectations led to disappointment, and hope was too fragile to risk.

I didn't have the language to speak these thoughts at the time, but deep inside, I made a silent promise to expect nothing, ask for nothing, and say nothing. It was my way of preventing pain and disappointment.

So, I learned how to float in the current, not with joy or a sense of adventure, but rather in silent resignation. For decades, from a teenager until sometime in my thirties, I let people, situations, and even fear chart my course. I thought a passive approach would bring peace; that apathy and detachment would protect me from pain. They didn't. They just numbed my heart and turned me into a spectator in my own story. Rather than living intentionally, I settled for a fearful, cautious existence, always waiting for the next wave to decide where I would drift.

My surrender didn't look all that dramatic from the outside. I chatted and smiled with others, and I met my obligations- school, work, and family functions. I said what I was supposed to say and acted well enough so that no one would suspect I carried such a heavy load. On the surface, I appeared happy and content, but inside, I was defeated. Not angry; just numb. Passive. Resigned.

I approached God in the same way. I believed that He was real, that He was ultimately in control and orchestrating all things. But I also convinced myself that He was out of reach and unapproachable. He was too big, too holy, and too uninterested in the details of my life to bother with me. In my mind, I constructed a God who was a distant dictator waiting to punish rather than a present Father longing to love.

Giving in kept pain at bay, but in the process, it reshaped my outlook until I forgot hope existed. I didn't realize He was truly near or that I could ever want more than a far-off God. I thought that if I could stay out of sight and obey the rules, I could survive this life and maybe sneak into heaven. So, I read the Bible out of obligation. But because I had closed God off, the words felt empty; the message detached. Miracles, mercy, and transformation were acts of God, but I was certain that such occurrences were meant for people holier, braver, or more important than me. As a result, reading the Bible became a chore, a box to be checked to avoid God's punishment.

The same was true of prayer; it was simply another requirement, an act of obedience to appease God that I hoped would bring me a little closer to heaven. I muttered muted words to a remote God, like a child reciting lines in a school play. I wished for approval but held no confidence that anyone actually heard my voice. I didn't speak boldly or listen intently. Rather, I prayed with my desires buried under years of disappointment, convinced of God's indifference.

And this passive floating became spiritual neglect, a state of lifelessness, not because I stopped believing but because I stopped searching. I pushed God away, and the slowly eroding powers of time and distraction turned my heart cold.

Take note: The shift is surprisingly subtle. Deceptively calm and quiet. You wake up and grab your phone instead of praying. You rush out of the house without acknowledging God. You convince yourself that you'll read later; you'll pray tomorrow. But tomorrow never comes, and one day-weeks or months later-you look into the mirror and see that your heart has become numb. Worship feels like a ritual; Scripture like mere history. Prayer has all but disappeared. You go to church, raise your hands, and say the right things while wondering when the fire went out-and why you didn't notice.

The descent into spiritual neglect isn't obvious. It doesn't announce its intent. Instead, it quietly suggests that your comfort outweighs conviction; that conversation with man overrules communion with God; and that control eclipses surrender. Neglect pulls the wool over your eyes, convincing you that nothing is amiss as you slowly slip away.

Yet in your numbness, in your silence, He is still there.

Not distant.

Not unreachable.

But waiting.

Like the father of the prodigal son, scouring the horizon for the wandering child. Not with arms folded to scold, but wide open to welcome.

And so, with the slightest turn of the heart, a single shed tear, or an earnest whisper that says, "I need You," and the gaping distance shrinks to almost nothing.

Because He was never far—only the fog of indifference gave the illusion of distance.

The truth is, God doesn't walk away; you and I do. But even in your wandering, He watches you, waiting for the moment you will turn back. Waiting for your heart to realize that numbness is not home.

He is.

A Shift Begins with a Spark

The change wasn't accompanied by a flamboyant explosion or angelic visit. There was no glorious illumination or shouting from heaven. Nothing obvious to signal a turning point.

Perhaps it began with a faint glimmer of yearning, brought on by years of rote religion and a life of empty belief that led my soul to wonder, *Is this all there is?* Or, out of quiet desperation, did my heart whisper, "Could there be more?"

But why the shift now? I did many things right: Church attendance. Prayer before meals. Tithing. Bible reading. Yet, these acts had become little more than muscle memory-a disciplined rhythm of religion without the pulsating breath of relationship. I believed in God, but I was not walking with Him. I did not look for Him. I did not expect Him to speak.

Yet, something within me was different. Something had changed. When I read my Bible, it was with a twinge of expectation, no longer to simply finish the passage but to hear from God. The once dead words seemed alive, as though reaching out to meet me. I prayed, not for help or a miracle, but for a connection-a holy echo to assure me that I wasn't just speaking into the air.

And with that ever-so-slight shift, a dim spark was lit. I began to understand that when you seek God, even cautiously, you begin to see Him.

Seeing What Was Already There

Romans 1:20 tells us: "For since the creation of the world God's invisible qualities-his eternal power and divine nature-have been clearly seen, being understood from what has been made, so that people are without excuse."

I told myself that God was not near, that He was a distant deity who presides over the universe from a faraway throne. I acknowledged His power and greatness, and even His work in the lives of other Christians. But I could not bring myself to believe that God could be in my kitchen or laundry room, in my weariness or worrying. I built a box and placed God neatly inside, out of sight.

Then came the spark, and I leaned in, just barely. I uttered a simple question that expressed a longing, and something incredible happened: I began to see His fingerprints all around me.

The moments that felt very ordinary suddenly shone with meaning. A conversation I nearly let slip away bore His whisper. A hymn that held no meaning brought a tear to my eye. The sincere smile of a stranger and an encouraging word from a friend all quietly proved His presence.

It was as if I lived in a world painted with divine brushstrokes but only now saw the colors. This promise of God became real to me: "The LORD is with you when you are with him. If you seek him, he will be found by you, but if you forsake him, he will forsake you." (2 Chronicles 15:2)

I could see it now. God had been there all along. The spark, ignited by the slightest yearning, had made Him visible.

That spark? Like neglect, it doesn't consume you all at once; rather, it is a small, steady flame in the very center of your being that lights what once was dark and warms what was bitterly cold. It is the light in your eye that confirms what your deeper understanding knows: He's here. He sees. He speaks.

From a desperate heart and a whisper came a spark that ignited new life-not one without difficulty or questions, but one marked by presence.

His presence.

Because when we turn from knowing *about* God to seeking to know Him, everything changes.

The Transformation

That faint flicker forged a new perspective. I began to see God differently, not as a vending machine for spiritual candies, but as my Father, my Counselor, and my Friend. My heart softened, not because I saw myself as holy, but because I became aware that the holiness of God was all around me.

Divine awareness shifted the purpose of my prayers from what I could get from God to simply wanting His presence. Words flowed from the heart, not simply read from a sterile list. I made fewer demands of "do this" or "heal them," and more petitions of "please be with me."

It was in that softening that I began to come alive and in the awareness that the transformation began. I felt an intensity, a hunger for God that my resignation and numbness had suppressed. And once His peace, His insight, His gentle nudging found a welcome home in me, I wanted more. More of Him, not things or even blessings. Just Him.

There was no straining to become a better version of myself. No pretending to be more faithful. Instead, change flowed from the deep revelation that He was already moving. He was already speaking and threading His presence through every chapter, page, and line of my life, patiently waiting for me to see Him and let Him in.

"Here I am! I stand at the door and knock. If anyone hears my voice and opens the door, I will come in and eat with that person, and they with me." (Revelation 3:20)

That invitation changes everything for me. I don't need to

chase Him down-I only need to open the door. Seeking isn't about effort; it's about response. It's about slowing down enough to hear the knock and being brave enough to let Him in.

And so, the discipline of seeking leads to the bliss of finding. What's more marvelous is that the God who created the universe does not wait for your perfection; He waits for your acknowledgment, for your slowing down, and for your leaning in.

And when you do, you realize that He was never too far. He was only waiting for you to adjust your sight.

From Despondence to Hope

When my focus shifted from myself to Him, something inside realigned, not suddenly or dramatically-just a quiet clarity that was steady and soft, like morning light gradually pushing the shadows away.

Then I began to see things in a new light. I found meaning-not in anything great or noble as the world would see it, but rather in the realization that somehow my life was not random. That my pain was not wasted. Those struggles and delays, those prayers that had seemingly never been answered, all existed within a larger tapestry; one that I could not yet see but was beginning to trust.

No longer was I just floating. I was being led.

Even when the destination was unknown.

Even when the journey didn't make sense.

Even when I felt the weight of pain and loss.

He was there.

And that truth was the only thing that gave me hope.

Hope my soul had always craved but refused to acknowledge.

Hope not based on good news or perfect timing-but eternal hope, the anchor for the soul.

Hope that keeps you company through uncertainty, whispering, "Even if nothing changes, I am still with you."

Hope that declares, "You are not invisible."

Hope that places identity in Christ, not in fears or failures.

And where true hope exists, despondence flees, and joy has room to breathe. Joy is not the shallow happiness that rests upon circumstances but the deep, settled delight that grows quietly in the soil of trust within. Joy doesn't erase sorrow but stands next to it, shouting, "Even here, even now, He is still good."

And where there is joy, peace is never far behind-a gentle friend, quietly filling the empty spaces once occupied by fear.

Friend, you will find that the result of welcoming God is this: your faith follows you not only in the important issues but also in the little ones; you find joy in daily chores and in the grocery aisle; and you find peace in your pain and struggles.

Do you see God in the early quietness of dawn and in the heavily silenced night? In the grief that lingers with questions unanswered?

When you no longer float but follow God, you realize that He was never absent. He was simply waiting to be welcomed in.

Life may never get easier, but in His presence, it becomes more sanctified. Ordinary activities turn into moments of communion. The mundane carries meaning. Your pain leaves you leaning on Him.

It is not a leap but a turn. A new narrative. A realignment of the soul. And it transforms everything. Because when your eyes glide from the edges of your limitations to His presence, you don't just find strength; you find Him. And in Him, you find everything that your heart has ever longed for.

The Ribbon, Unboxed

A ribbon that once lay boxed and forgotten in the shadows of a dusty attic and neglected soul, today sits in sacred, meaningful light, not because of its transformation, but because of mine. I no longer see it as worn, faded fabric. I see a testimony, a reminder that carries me back to when I was adrift, going through the motions of faith but without its substance. It was easy for God to be just background noise-existing but displaced, set aside, and boxed up like that ribbon, waiting to be remembered.

The comfort of spiritual neglect is a subtle thief. It does not announce itself through chaos. It slithers in, convincing you that drifting is safe because it is slow and convenient. Until one day, you wake up to discover a spiritual void, not because you ran, but because you no longer reach out.

The ribbon is a symbol of that truth. It reminds me that spiritual neglect steals not only intimacy with God but also hope, joy, purpose, and identity.

However, it also cautions me that spiritual awakening is a gift not always opened at a revival meeting or during a mountaintop encounter. Sometimes, the gift appears as a simple whisper of hunger, a change in focus, or a resolution to stop drifting and start listening again.

That is exactly what the ribbon signifies for me: a tangible marker of a spiritual awakening. It sits where I see it often, not as a relic of the past but as a promise for the present. A visible reminder that I'm not here to float. I'm here to follow.

Follow the voice that speaks in stillness.

Follow the Shepherd who leaves the ninety-nine for the one.

Follow the Father who didn't wait for me to be worthy but called to me while I was still wandering.

So don't box God in. Don't confine Him to the corners of your life where it's convenient or socially acceptable. Don't reserve Him just for Sunday mornings or desperate prayers.

Invite Him to the Center

Welcome God into your to-do list, the dusty corners of your regrets, your moments of laughter, and your plain old days, where the sacred is often smothered by the mundane.

Let Him shift your gaze. Let Him light a spark that will awaken your soul. Because here is the truth, though you might not want to hear it: God has never turned His face from you. Not once has He tuned out your cries. Never has He stopped writing beautiful chapters of redemption into your story, even the chapters you wanted to skip.

Acknowledge the signs of God's presence all around you: the kindness of a stranger, the Scripture that answers your nagging question, peace that engulfs you when your entire world crumbles.

Because when everything else fades away, His presence is constant. With that realization, transformation can begin. And I have a ribbon to remind me of that truth.

Reflection

"The LORD is with you when you are with him. If you seek him, he will be found by you, but if you forsake him, he will forsake you."

(2 Chronicles 15:2)

"Again and again they put God to the test; they vexed the Holy One of Israel."

(Psalm 78:41)

Q: What is stirred in your heart when you hear the promise, "The LORD is with you when you are with Him"?

_____

_____

_____

(Please continue in your own journal!)

Q: In what areas of your life are you actively seeking Him-and in what areas are you floating, assuming His presence without truly pursuing Him?

_____

_____

_____

(Please continue in your own journal!)

Q: Are you limiting God by boxing Him into your ways and timing? How might seeking Him openly transform you?

_____

_____

_____

(Please continue in your own journal!)

Q: What would it look like to release your expectations and trust that if you seek Him, you will find Him-even if He leads you somewhere unexpected or uncomfortable?

_____

_____

_____

(Please continue in your own journal!)

Prayer

Heavenly Father,

I confess that I've spent too many seasons drifting-believing in You but not engaging with You. Forgive me for the times I boxed You in, limiting where and how I allowed You to move in my life.

Today, I choose to awaken. I want to see You in the ordinary and hear You in the quiet. Stir in me a hunger for Your presence.

Give me the courage to look for You, the patience to wait on You, and the boldness to obey You.

Let my life be a ribbon unboxed, visible, sacred, and fully surrendered to Your purpose.

In Jesus' name, Amen.

Epilogue:
The Thread That Holds

As I end this journey, I marvel at the fact that God entrusted this project, this book, to me.

Me? An ordinary person with no theological pedigree or fancy credentials. Just a willing heart with lots of questions.

But that's just it, isn't it? God is not looking for perfection. He is looking for permission. And when you offer it, however timidly, He steps in and begins to do what only He can: bring purpose out of uncertainty, clarity out of chaos, and meaning out of moments that once felt too ordinary to matter.

I have fallen short before-many times. Even when the Holy Spirit nudged (or, let's be honest, shoved) me, I walked away. I quit on God. But this time, I stayed. I obeyed. I didn't write because I had all the answers; I wrote because I finally accepted the invitation to wrestle.

And that wrestling? That is exactly what Jude 3 calls for. To contend for the faith. To press in and stay engaged in a world that tries to water down truth, twist grace, and distract you with false gospels.

Jude's letter is not a casual commentary. He wrote with a sense of urgency. The term "contend" comes from ancient wrestling, which is a gritty, physical, and continuous endeavor.

Not a one-time act but a discipline for a lifetime. Not passive faith. This is active, alert, grounded, and aware.

The challenge is the same now as it was then: deception surrounds us, truth is under siege, and temptations abound. Yet you are not left unarmed. God will always equip you for the battle.

In my case, the weapons came in the form of a simple ribbon and reminders that turned my heart and my eyes back to Him. And that simple turn brought everything into focus. I recognized that I had become complacent, settled in my routine with God. I worshipped, I studied, I sought His guidance, but only within my comfort zone. In some distant corner of my mind, I had already decided just how far I was willing to go with Him.

And it hit me: though I wasn't shutting God completely out as I had in the past, I was placing limits on Him. I was still putting Him in a box-it was just a bigger box!

That stung, but from the pain of that realization came a steadfast conviction. Courage and determination I'd never known before were planted in my soul. Now, when anger rises up, I don't act; I remember: He is there. When disappointment comes, rather than shrink, I remember: He is there. I see the ribbon and its message:

- Your sins are covered by Christ's blood.

- You are a co-heir with Christ.

- Be yielding and moldable, willing to do God's work.

- Imperfection does not disqualify you.

- God can always be found.

- God is never finished with you.

- Do not be deceived; be prepared.

- Don't ignore God.

There was no conscious decision to change, yet I have changed. No, God *is changing* me. Because of the ribbon, I no longer flee for protection; I reach out for connection. And at the other end of a thread of hope, I find a faithful Father. One who never walked away but waited.

These reminders are not just weapons; they are anchors. And for me, a ribbon has become the symbol of that anchoring presence.

It had been there for years, tucked away in its own little box-quite easy to overlook-but now it sits in a place of prominence, where it can be clearly seen. It reminds me that God was always there. Even in the silence. Even in my questions. Even when I thought I had nothing to offer.

The ribbon tells the truth: He still holds the thread.

So, I ask you: What is the ribbon in your life? What slight, almost insignificant thing is God using to whisper in your ear?

Ask Him, "Lord, open my eyes. Awaken my heart to Your voice in the ordinary."

Now look carefully. He is not merely at the finish line, but with you in each stage of the journey. He is in your errands, in your struggles, in your pain. And when you forget, He is waiting somewhere along your path for you to perceive His presence, not with condemnation, but with rejoicing.

Because guess what? He never left. Like that ribbon, He was always there.

Always waiting. Always weaving. Always holding the thread.

So, what are you waiting for? Reach out and grasp it!

With Love and Faith,

Pam

About the Author

Are you contending for the faith or resting on your blessed assurance? Pamela has been in both camps. As a Christian for forty-five years and a Sunday School teacher for over twenty years, she has experienced all the phases: on fire, cold as ice, complacent, and even lukewarm. She has ridden the nauseating roller coaster of fierce faith followed by despondent doubt. With her gaze now firmly fixed on Christ, she seeks to help others by sharing the lessons she has learned.

Pamela is a proud Air Force veteran who considers her greatest accomplishments to be her forty-one-year marriage, her two children, and her six grandchildren. As an avid football fan, she admittedly allows her team's success or failure to affect her disposition-so much so that she recently declared a football "fast."

After calling several states home, Pamela and her husband settled in Gloucester County, Virginia. She enjoys being on the water, travelling, and spending time with friends and family.